TURNING THE TIDE AT GETTYSBURG

TURNING THE TIDE AT
GETTYSBURG

HOW MAINE SAVED THE UNION

★ JERRY R. DESMOND ★

DownEastBooks
CAMDEN, MAINE

Down East Books

Published by Down East Books
A wholly owned subsidiary of The Rowman & Littlefield Publishing Group, Inc.
4501 Forbes Boulevard, Suite 200, Lanham, Maryland 20706
www.rowman.com

16 Carlisle Street, London W1D 3BT, United Kingdom

Distributed by NATIONAL BOOK NETWORK

British Library Cataloguing in Publication Information Available
Library of Congress Cataloging-in-Publication Data Available

ISBN 978-1-60893-274-0 (paperback : alk. paper)
ISBN 978-1-60893-275-7 (electronic)

♾™ The paper used in this publication meets the minimum requirements of
American National Standard for Information Sciences—Permanence of Paper for
Printed Library Materials, ANSI/NISO Z39.48-1992.

Printed in the United States of America

Table of *CONTENTS*

PREFACE

Recently, it seems, a trend is developing in the prefaces of newly published works about the Battle of Gettysburg. The authors are writing brief apologies for adding yet another book on some aspect of the battle. Some have reason to do so, having very little to add to the story. There will be no apologies forthcoming from this author. Here's why.

The American Civil War and the Battle of Gettysburg have fascinated the reading public since almost as soon as the war ended in 1865. The Library of Congress lists 84,207 items about the war in its collection, almost 3,000 of which have been added in the last decade. It is estimated that there have been more than 60,000 books, articles, and other manuscripts written about the American Civil War in the past 150 years. Almost half of them have been about this single engagement fought on the first three days of July in 1863. When doing a Google search on line for Gettysburg, seven million results appear in a fifth of a second about the battle, more than three times the number for the Battle of Vicksburg, the other so-called great turning point battle of that momentous year in American History.

Why is Gettysburg more popular than any other battle or topic of the war? There are several reasons. Gettysburg was the largest single battle ever fought in North America. Over 160,000 men engaged in combat in or near this small town in Pennsylvania. Almost one third of them became casualties, the highest number of casualties in one battle of the four year war, almost eight times the casualties suffered by American forces on D-Day in World War II. Any time something is the greatest or the biggest it is bound to become famous. Amateur and professional historians alike have been compelled to explore and analyze the battle to its smallest detail. To add to the record, the Gettysburg campaign certainly has more first-person accounts than any other campaign of the Civil War. It is amazing how many letters, diaries, etc., have found the light of day since the battle's centennial in 1963.

The stakes at the time of the battle were extremely high — a smashing Confederate victory may have resulted in independence for the southern states. Following the battle, the success of the Confederate cause in the war became less likely. For southerners at the time, and even today, the Battle of Gettysburg became the "Big If," a symbol of how close the "Lost Cause" came to success. What if Stonewall Jackson had been there on the first day? What if J.E.B. Stuart had kept his cavalry in closer contact with Lee's army? What if Longstreet had attacked four hours earlier on the second day? What if the Confederate army had been victorious at Gettysburg? In the moments before Pickett's Charge on the third day of the battle, it seemed Southern independence was only three quarters of a mile away. It became mythologized as the "High Water Mark" of the war, even though the real apogee of Confederate success occurred several months before in September of 1862 when Lee's Army of Northern Virginia invaded Maryland and Bragg's Army of Tennessee dashed (if it is possible to use the word dash and Bragg in the same sentence) into Kentucky. To cement the myth, a High Water Mark of the Rebellion Monument was placed on Cemetery Ridge in Gettysburg in 1892 with an inscription identifying Pickett's Charge as "unquestionably the high water mark of this battle, and of the war!"

In addition, the town, in November of 1863, became the site of the most famous speech in American history — Lincoln's Gettysburg Address. The effort begun there by President Lincoln to memorialize the battle eventually resulted in the site becoming a symbol of reconciliation between the two halves of the country. Civil War veterans flocked to Gettysburg over the next 75 years to attend reunions both Union and Confederate. By 1913, the 50th anniversary of the battle, the reunions had combined into one large encampment capped by a speech from the first elected southern President of the United States since Zachary Taylor. President Woodrow Wilson (born in Virginia four years before the Civil War) on July 4, 1913 summarized the spirit of those gathered: "We have found one another again as brothers and comrades in arms, enemies no longer, generous friends rather, our battles long past, the quarrel forgotten—except that we shall not forget the splendid valor." In 1938, President Franklin Roosevelt dedicated the Eternal Light Peace Memorial on Oak Hill with the inscription "Peace Eternal in a Nation United."

Perhaps most important, Gettysburg was the only major battle fought in a non-slave state. As such, it is the closest battle to the large population and media centers of the country. Philadelphia is only two-and-a-half hours away by car today. New York City is about four hours away. Even at the turn of the last century, the battle site was reachable by train in less than a couple days. So it became the most logical place for states, especially northern states, to first build monuments to commemorate their soldiers' sacrifices and courage during the war. It has become the Mecca of Civil War battlefields. Today, about three million people visit Gettysburg each year to gaze at the statues and retrace the steps of Generals Lee and Meade, Stuart and Hancock, Longstreet and Chamberlain, and their own great-great-great grandfathers.

My Gettysburg saga began on a family trip in June 1972. My very talented sister, Ronnee Beth, had been selected for the All-U.S.A. chorus and band, two members so honored from every state, for a traveling tour of Europe. The meeting place for rehearsal and departure for the group was Shenandoah College in Winchester, Virginia, (the most contested town in America, it changed hands more than seventy times during the Civil War). My father, a high school history teacher in Presque Isle, Maine, and a huge Civil War buff, saw this as a chance to check off a list of historical places he had never visited. So he loaded up the family into a 1969 Ford Galaxie station wagon and we headed out of New England for the first time in our lives. By the time we got to Gettysburg, we were way behind schedule, so we did a quick driving tour, never getting out of the car. The monuments whizzed by as we sped out of town on our way to Virginia. On the ride back home we gave Washington, D.C., the same treatment, arriving and leaving on the same day burglars broke into the Democratic National Committee headquarters at the Watergate office complex.

I did not return to Gettysburg until another, more relaxed family visit in 1990. By this time Michael Shaara's book, *The Killer Angels* had been published and Ken Burns' *The Civil War* film documentary had just been broadcast on PBS. The biggest hero of these works, it seemed to me and others, was Joshua Chamberlain, a college professor from Maine and defender of Little Round Top at Gettysburg. He became one of the most admired and famous generals of the conflict. So the highlight of this trip was a pilgrimage to the site of the 20th Maine monument. Thus inspired, the following year I moved south, first to finally get away from cold weather (where I am from in Northern Maine there is only one day of summer — July 10th from 2:00-4:00 pm), and second, to be closer to Civil War battlefields (except for a small bank robbery in Calais and a few off-shore naval engagements, there are no Civil War battlefields in Maine. It was all mainly hosted in the South).

While taking several museum jobs in Tennessee and Georgia over the next decade, I traveled by car to almost all of the major Civil War sites (except Pea Ridge, Arkansas). I would also go home to Northern Maine two or three times a year to see the family and remind myself about the weather. Gettysburg turned out to be almost exactly half way on the 1,400 mile trip. So the visits began to pile up.

Then, in 1999, I was hired to be the lead curatorial consultant for the new National Civil War Museum built in Harrisburg, Pennsylvania. As such I not only was responsible for the cataloging of a $15 million collection of Civil War artifacts but also in providing label text and selecting photographs for the museum exhibits (visitors to the museum today may wonder why a museum in Pennsylvania has such a large number of Maine-related photographs and wall murals on display). Over the next three years, every chance I could get, I would drive the 35 miles down Rte. 15 from Harrisburg to the Gettysburg battlefield, sometimes for a morning or an afternoon and sometimes for an entire weekend.

When the job was done, I kept coming back (in 2013, I made my 108th visit to Gettysburg). Getting deeper into the story of those three days in 1863, I began to notice that at each critical point of the battlefield a Maine regiment played an important role in defending Union soil. The battle, it turned out, was not just about Joshua Chamberlain and the 20th Maine regiment. Hall's 2nd Maine Battery on the Chambersburg Pike, the 16th Maine on Oak Ridge, the 3rd Maine in the Peach Orchard, the 17th Maine in the Wheatfield, Stevens's 5th Maine Battery on Culp's Hill, the 4th Maine in Devil's Den, and the 19th Maine on Cemetery Ridge all performed pivotal roles in the battle. Dow's 6th Maine Battery, the 5th Maine regiment, 6th Maine Regiment, 7th Maine regiment, 10th Maine Battalion, 1st Maine Cavalry, and Company D (Maine) of the 2nd U.S. Sharpshooters also provided excellent service and support. New heroes emerged — Captain James Hall, Lieutenant Colonel Charles Tilden, Captain Greenlief

General Oliver Otis Howard

Stevens, General Oliver Otis Howard, Colonel Freeman McGilvery, among others.

In fact, the 4,022 Maine men who fought at Gettysburg performed at a level much higher than their numbers should indicate; almost 1,000 of them became casualties. Being only 4.3% of the entire Union Army, men from Maine received 7.9% of the Medals of Honor awarded for bravery during the battle. Of all of the Northern States represented there with over 3% of the army, Maine received the highest number of Medals of Honor per 1,000 soldiers at 1.24 medals, or one Medal of Honor for every 804 soldiers. In comparison, men from the State of New York, representing over one-fourth of the Union army, received only .44 Medals of Honor per 1,000 soldiers, or one Medal of Honor for every 2,302 soldiers. This at least indicates that Maine men found themselves in some hot spots during the battle and performed admirably.[1]

There are some very good books about individual Maine regiments that are entirely about or have chapters about the battle. Tom Desjardins, the current historian for Maine's Department of Agriculture, Conservation and Forestry, is the author of *Stand Firm Ye Boys From Maine: The 20th Maine and the Gettysburg Campaign*, an excellent study of the mythology of Joshua Chamberlain. John J. Pullen's *The Twentieth Maine* is still the standard for any regimental history of the Civil War. William B. Jordan's book, *Red Diamond Regiment, The 17th Maine Regiment*, has an enlightening chapter about the regiment's fight in the Wheatfield. James H. Mundy has written books about the 2nd Maine Regiment (some of the men from this regiment were combined into the 20th Maine and fought at Gettysburg) and the 6th Maine Regiment. In fact, the Maine State

Medal of Honor Recipients Comparison — Battle of Gettysburg

States with more than 3% of the Total Union Army

State	Percentage of Union Army at Gettysburg	Percentage of Medal of Honor Recipients at Gettysburg	Medals of Honor per 1,000 troops at Gettysburg
Maine	4.3%	7.9%	1.24
Massachusetts	6.5%	11.1%	1.21
Vermont	4.8%	6.3%	0.96
Pennsylvania	26.1%	31.8%	0.85
Ohio	4.9%	4.8%	0.68
New York	25.7%	15.9%	0.44
Michigan	3.0%	0.0%	0.00
New Jersey	4.5%	0.0%	0.00
All Other Troops	20.5%	22.2%	0.96

Library listed only eighty-eight works about Maine's role in the Civil War in a selected bibliography of material published in honor of the Civil War Sesquicentennial in 2011.

Therefore, the total number of monographs about Maine at Gettysburg, and even Maine during the Civil War, is fairly small in comparison with the impact on the outcome of the battle and the war by men from Maine. In fact, except for *Maine at Gettysburg,* a 602 page book published in 1898 for the State of Maine by the Maine Gettysburg Commissioner's Executive Committee, there has been no comprehensive study of Maine regiments at Gettysburg in the past 115 years.

So, again, there will be no apology for publishing this book about Maine at Gettysburg from this author. There will only be thanks for those who There will only be thanks for those who provided much needed assistance in compiling information, images and support. These include the fabulous staff at the Maine State Archives in Augusta, especially Dan Cheever, the Maine State Archivist and Peter Mallow at the Imaging Center. Bill Cook, the History and Special Collections Librarian at the Bangor Public Library and Holly Hurd-Forsyth, the registrar at the Maine Historical Society in Portland also were very helpful. Margot Carpenter of Hartdale Maps in Belfast was extremely patient and precise as she designed the maps for this book. Virginia (Ginny) Wright, Senior Editor at *Down East* magazine, who edited the original article in the July, 2013 edition of the magazine which led to this book, is simply awesome. Michael Steere, of Down East Books, gets full credit for the wonderful layout of the book and its careful editing. I am grateful for his professionalism and patience. I took my good friend John Larson and his family (Judy, Amy, and John, Jr.) on a Maine tour of Gettysburg in the mid-1990s, which planted the first thought in my head that someone needs to write a book about the topic.

A shout out goes to my 8th grade history teacher, Mr. Robert (Bob) Carter and my high school history teacher, Ms. Dorothy Dingwall, for inspiring a career in history. Of course, no one provided more inspiration than my father, Jerry R. Desmond, Sr. (1930-2007), to whom this book is dedicated, In Memoriam.

NOTES

1. The subtitle of this book, "How Maine Saved the Union," is in no way meant to disparage the fighting qualities of the other 89,000 men in the Union Army. They did not just stand back and watch the Maine regiments do all of the fighting. Over half of the Union army came from New York and Pennsylvania, so those states certainly contributed to the cause. Once when asked why the South lost the Battle of Gettysburg, Confederate General George Pickett replied, ""I always thought the Yankees had something to do with it." He did not mean just Maine Yankees, of course, but he could have.

LEGEND

	Union		Confederate
	SICKLES	Corps	**A.P. HILL**
	ROBINSON	Division	RODES
	CUTLER'S BRIGADE	Brigade	**DAVIS' BRIGADE**

  Regiment Advancing

  Regiment Retreating

  Regiment in Position

  Battery

■   Point of Interest

═══   Road, Pike

▦▦▦   Railroad

▦▦▦   Unfinished Railroad

～～   Waterway

Forest

Contour Interval for Overview Maps = 10 Feet
Contour Interval for Battle Maps = 5 Feet

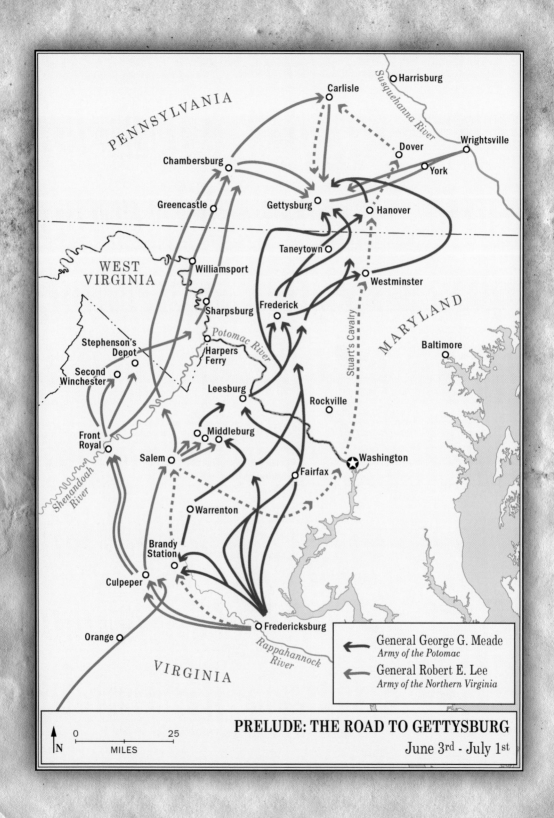

PENNSYLVANIA

WEST VIRGINIA

MARYLAND

VIRGINIA

Harrisburg

Carlisle

Susquehanna River

Dover

Wrightsville

Chambersburg

York

Greencastle

Gettysburg

Hanover

Taneytown

Williamsport

Westminster

Sharpsburg

Frederick

Potomac River

Stephenson's Depot

Baltimore

Harpers Ferry

Second Winchester

Stuart's Cavalry

Leesburg

Rockville

Front Royal

Middleburg

Salem

Washington

Shenandoah River

Fairfax

Warrenton

Brandy Station

Culpeper

Orange

Fredericksburg

Rappahannock River

←	**General George G. Meade** *Army of the Potomac*
←	**General Robert E. Lee** *Army of the Northern Virginia*

0   25
MILES
N

PRELUDE: THE ROAD TO GETTYSBURG
June 3rd - July 1st

THE ROAD TO GETTYSBURG

T he situation for Confederate forces and their cause in late May of 1863 looked bleak. Both Vicksburg and Port Hudson on the Mississippi River were under siege and in danger of falling. The Army of Tennessee, under General Braxton Bragg, had retreated to Tullahoma, Tennessee, following the Battle of Stone's River, where Bragg faced a near mutiny of subordinate generals (within a month the Army of Tennessee would retreat almost out of its namesake state to the Georgia border at Chattanooga). Three of the eleven Confederate state capitals had been captured — Nashville, Tennessee, Baton Rouge, Louisiana, and Jackson, Mississippi. In addition, the Union naval blockade of southern ports had tightened, effectively strangling commerce including foreign supplies of arms, food, and medical supplies.

To relieve the pressure, Confederate President Jefferson F. Davis, and others in the southern government, wanted General Robert E. Lee to release a portion of the Army of Northern Virginia to the western theater, especially to aid in the breaking of the siege of Vicksburg. Resisting this plan, Lee turned his thoughts to another invasion of the northern states. With the return of General James Longstreet's 1st corps from foraging duty near Suffolk, Virginia, Lee made up the losses incurred during the Battle of Chancellorsville in early May of 1863. He now had over 70,000 men, which he reorganized into three corps, each corps divided into three divisions — 1st Corps under General Longstreet, 2nd Corps now led by General Richard S. Ewell (following the death of General Thomas "Stonewall" Jackson on May 10, 1863) and 3rd Corps led by the sickly General Ambrose P. Hill.

THE ARMY OF NORTHERN VIRGINIA	CORPS STRENGTH
Longstreet's First Corps	20,706
Ewell's Second Corps	20,666
Hill's Third Corps	22,083
Stuart's Cavalry	6,621
Total	**70,076**

General Lee believed his invasion plan could accomplish several objectives. First, an invasion north into Pennsylvania, with threats toward Washington, D.C., Baltimore, and Philadelphia, might force President Lincoln to transfer troops from Vicksburg and Tennessee to protect these cities. Second, an invasion would allow Virginia farmers to recover their fields and harvest crops, especially in the Shenandoah Valley, relieving somewhat the Confederacy's supply problems. It would also be an opportunity for the Army of Northern Virginia to forage for badly needed supplies in the rich agricultural areas of Pennsylvania. Finally, an overwhelming victory by southern arms in the North might provide an excuse for foreign recognition and aid, especially by the British and the French.

Notwithstanding a couple of negative votes, President Davis and his advisors approved Lee's plan at a strategic conference in Richmond. On June 3, 1863, General Lee ordered General Longstreet to begin the movement of his corps to the west from its base near Fredericksburg, Virginia, instructing General J. E. B. Stuart to use his cavalry to screen this movement from observation by Union troops. Lee's plan was to move west and then north up the Shenandoah Valley to cross the Potomac River at points near Shepherdstown, Maryland. The goal was to draw the Army of the Potomac out in the open where it could be destroyed. A prime objective would be the capture of Harrisburg, Pennsylvania, a major rail center and link between the Atlantic states and the Midwest, and the destruction of a key railroad bridge across the Susquehanna River at Wrightsville, Pennsylvania.

To oppose this invasion, the Army of the Potomac, under the command of Major General Joseph Hooker, had over 93,000 troops, divided in to seven corps, a cavalry corps, and an artillery reserve. This force included about 4,000 Maine men organized in nine regiments, three artillery batteries, one cavalry regiment, one battalion serving as provost guards and one company of sharpshooters.

As Lee's forces moved up the Shenandoah Valley, General Ewell's corps took the lead, recapturing Winchester, Virginia, by June 14 and crossing the Mason-Dixon Line into Pennsylvania on June 22. Reacting slowly to this movement, General Hooker finally got the Army of the Potomac moving into Maryland on June 25, as the 1st Corps, 3rd Corps, and 11th Corps crossed the Potomac at Edward's Ferry, some thirty miles to the northwest of Washington, D.C., their objective being to seize Crampton's and Turner's Gaps on South Mountain.

The march of over 140 miles from a base north of Fredericksburg on the Rappahannock River to Gettysburg in the heat of the southern summer was especially hard on the men from Maine. The 20th Maine began its march north on June 13. For the next four days, the weather turned especially hot, climbing into the 90s, the worst day being a march of eighteen miles on the June 17. Colonel Chamberlain came down with partial

ARMY OF THE POTOMAC	NUMBER ENGAGED	NUMBER MAINE ENGAGED
General Staff (Hooker)	11	2[1]
Headquarters	1,732[2]	0
1st Corps (Reynolds)	12,222	538
2nd Corps (Hancock)	11,347	406
3rd Corps (Sickles)	10,675	919
5th Corps (Meade)	10,907	386
6th Corps (Sedgwick)	13,596	1,041
11th Corps (Howard)	9,188	2[3]
12th Corps (Slocum)	9,788	205
Cavalry (Pleasonton)	11,851	419
Artillery Reserve (Tyler)	2,376	104
Total	**93,693**[4]	**4,022**[5]

1. Brigadier General Seth Williams and Brigadier General Rufus Ingalls.

2. Along with the General Staff, the Army of the Potomac headquarters including men from the 93rd New York regiment, the 8th U.S. regiment, the 2nd and 6th Pennsylvania Cavalry regiments and the Oneida Independent Cavalry Company of New York.

3. Major General Oliver O. Howard and Brigadier General Adelbert Ames.

4. Various corps and regimental numbers are found in several sources, these listed are from the author's own calculations. However, they are hard numbers to pin down and should not be considered exact. In the 4th edition of Regiment Losses and Strengths at Gettysburg by John W. Busey and David G. Martin (2005), the total engaged strength of the Army of the Potomac is listed as 93,921. They list Lee's Army of Northern Virginia's engaged strength at 71,699, for a total engaged strength of 165,620.

5. At full strength these Maine regiments would total about 11,000 men, which illustrates how much these units had already lost during the war's first two years.

sunstroke, which kept him out of action during a brief fight with Confederate cavalry on June 19 near Middleburg, Virginia. In the five days between June 26 and July 1, the regiment covered 107 miles, before going into a reserve position along the Baltimore Pike just to the southeast of the town of Gettysburg.

The other Maine regiments had similar experiences. The 3rd Corps (including the 3rd, 4th, and 17th Maine regiments) began its march north on June 11. Passing the old Bull Run battlefield on June 16, the 3rd Corps, after three days of idleness, made a leisurely pace to Gum Springs, Maryland. On June 25, the corps covered 35 miles in about seventeen hours, much of the march in heavy rain, crossing the Monocacy River early the next day. Over the next few days, the corps marched north via Frederick and Taneytown, Maryland. By then, the command of the Army of the Potomac had undergone a startling change and the pace of events quickened.

On June 28, General Hooker was replaced by order of President Lincoln with Major General George Meade. On this date, all of Lee's army was in Pennsylvania, with Longstreet's Corps and Hill's Corps near Chambersburg and two of Ewell's divisions at Carlisle (just a one-day march from that railroad bridge and Harrisburg) and one division at York. Stuart's Cavalry had finally crossed the Potomac River, but to the east of Union forces and thus not in contact with the rest of Lee's army (and now further encumbered by 125 captured wagons). Meade's army was still in Maryland along the Monocacy River near Frederick, with the 6th Corps twenty miles to the south. Units of the Federal cavalry had crossed the state line into Pennsylvania and were camped about ten miles from Gettysburg.

That night, General Lee was informed by a Confederate scout that the Union army was on the move and closing. This forced Lee on June 29 to cancel Ewell's attack on Harrisburg and order his army to concentrate at Cashtown, about eight miles to the northwest from Gettysburg. On June 30, Brigadier General John Buford's First Division of the Union cavalry corps entered Gettysburg, setting up a defensive line on the Chambersburg Pike to the west of the town. Confederate General Henry Heth, now at Cashtown, was directed by General A.P. Hill to take his division of Hill's Corps east towards Gettysburg the next day to scout and procure supplies, under orders to not bring on a general engagement. The Battle of Gettysburg was about to unfold.

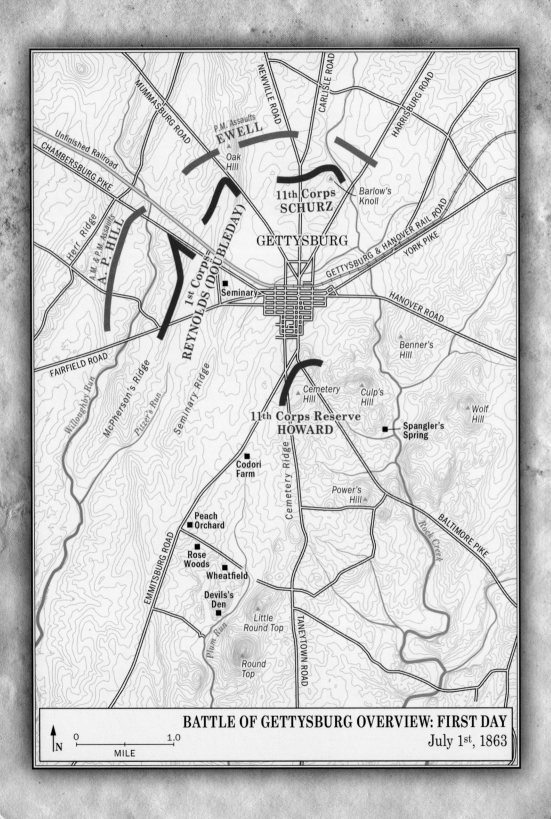

BATTLE OF GETTYSBURG OVERVIEW: FIRST DAY
July 1st, 1863

DAY ONE
July 1, 1863
THE BATTLE BEGINS

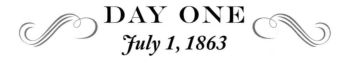

As the dawn of July 1, 1863 broke in Gettysburg, the rains of the previous day and evening had moved on to the east. At 7:00 a.m., Reverend Dr. Michael Jacobs, a math professor at what was then called Pennsylvania College (now Gettysburg College), recorded the temperature as a mild 72 degrees, with overcast gray clouds and a slight two m.p.h. breeze coming from the south. It was a typical summer's day in central Pennsylvania, except . . . that it was not.

To the west of town, along the Chambersburg Pike, Union cavalry under the command of General John Buford had taken a position near the McPherson farm with videttes (lookouts) posted further west on Herr's Ridge. With about 2,700 troopers, Buford would soon face the 7,600 men of Confederate General Henry Heth's division of Hill's 3rd Corps, moving east along the pike.

The Battle of Gettysburg began as a meeting engagement. It was unusual because the Southern army approached the town from the north and west, while the Northern army came to the scene from the south and east. It was also unusual because the Confederate troops were advancing without a cavalry screen. General Heth, therefore, had no idea of the character or strength of the Union force facing him. Outnumbered almost three to one, Buford's men held off the Confederates long enough for the 1st Corps of Major General John Reynolds to march into battle line sometime near 10:00 a.m. With over 12,000 men, including the renowned Iron Brigade, Reynolds' men were able to stop the Confederate advance. However, General Reynolds was killed by a sniper and command of the 1st Corps fell to General Abner Doubleday.

Hearing the sounds of battle, Confederate General Richard Ewell's 2nd Corps advanced south on the Carlisle Road to Oak Hill, finding itself in the early afternoon on the right flank of the Union 1st Corps. It also faced the newly arrived Union 11th Corps, which had taken position north of the town of Gettysburg, under the command of Major-General Oliver O. Howard (of Leeds, Maine). Assuming command of all Union troops then at Gettysburg, General Howard established a fall back defensive line at Cemetery Hill, a prominent spot just south of town.

Major General Oliver Otis Howard — The Christian General

The tiny town of Leeds, Maine, produced three Civil War generals — Oliver Otis Howard, his brother Charles Howard, and Confederate General Danville Leadbetter (who probably was most responsible for Union victories at Missionary Ridge and Knoxville during the Civil War, due to his faulty placement of Confederate lines). Oliver O. Howard, a graduate of both Bowdoin College (1850) and West Point (1854), reached the highest rank of any Maine native during the Civil War. During Sherman's Georgia, South Carolina, and North Carolina campaigns, Howard served as the commander of the Army of the Tennessee. He lost his left arm at the Battle of Fair Oaks in 1862 in an action for which he later was awarded the Medal of Honor.

Following the war, he headed the Freedman's Bureau, fought Indians out west, helped found Howard University in Washington, D.C., and Lincoln Memorial University in Harrogate, Tennessee, and wrote several books about his campaigns. A fanatical prohibitionist and evangelical, traits which annoyed both his superiors and those who fought under him, he became known as the "Christian General."

His leadership of the 11th Corps during the Battles of Chancellorsville and Gettysburg has come under much criticism by historians of the period. While some of this is earned, much is due to unfavorable circumstances. At Gettysburg, Howard actually performed professionally with some degree of competence. Taking command of the battlefield at the death of General John Reynolds on July 1, 1863, Howard quickly realized that Cemetery Hill was the key position on the field. He ably organized a strong reserve there, for this he received the Thanks of Congress.

A favorite story about Howard involves Colonel William C. Oates, the leader of the 15th Alabama that was defeated by Chamberlain's 20th Maine at Little Round Top. At the dedication ceremony of the Chickamauga battlefield in 1895, Oates gave an angry and rambling speech about states' rights which was not well received. After the ceremony, Howard, who was there on the grandstand, made his way over to Oates, put his one good arm around him and said, "I know how you feel."

Quick quiz — Who was older at the Battle of Gettysburg — Oliver O. Howard or Joshua Chamberlain?

Answer: Chamberlain, in charge of a regiment of about 350 men, was 35. Howard, who was in charge of 26 regiments and five batteries of artillery totaling about 9.000 men, was just 32 years old, by far the youngest corps commander in the army.

With the arrival of General Robert E. Lee on the battlefield, both Hill's and Ewell's Corps were ordered to attack, forcing the Union troops to retreat through the town after more than eight hours of determined fighting. As nightfall approached, General Ewell decided to not attempt an attack on Cemetery Hill or to move to capture Culp's Hill.

The first day of the Battle of Gettysburg had been an overwhelming Confederate victory, although casualties had been heavy. Maine units that participated in the first day's fight included Hall's 2nd Maine Battery, the 16th Maine Regiment and Stevens's 5th Maine Battery. Brigadier General Adelbert Ames, of Rockland, Maine, took charge of the 1st Division of the 11th Corps upon the wounding of the division's commander, General Francis Barlow.

Adelbert Ames — A Sharp Lead–er

Born in Rockland, Maine, the son of a sea captain, Adelbert Ames was only 21 years old when the Civil War started. Graduating fifth in his class at West Point in May of 1861, Ames was badly wounded in the leg at the First Battle of Bull Run (for which he was awarded the Medal of Honor in 1894). Returning to Maine he was appointed as the Colonel of the newly formed 20th Maine regiment, which he led until being promoted after the Battle of Chancellorsville to Brigadier General, taking over a brigade in the 11tn Corps.

Following the wounding and capture of General Barlow on the first day at Gettysburg, Ames took command of the First Division of the 11th Corps, leading its retreat through the town of Gettysburg to Cemetery Hill. There he performed well during the next two days of fighting, actually taking part in hand-to-hand combat at one point. As a token of esteem, the 20th Maine presented him with their battle flag when the battle was over.

Ames fought in several more engagements during the war (he should have received a second Medal of Honor for leading the charge at the Second Battle of Fort Fisher) and ended the war with a Brevet Major Generalship. Following the war, he married General Benjamin Butler's daughter, became the much-hated reconstruction governor and senator of Mississippi, fought in the Spanish-American War in Cuba, and became the last surviving full rank general of the Civil War, finally dying in 1933 at the age of 97.

Oh, and by the way, in 1890, Ames received U.S. Patent number 442,485 for inventing a lead pencil sharpener.

"THE BOYS FOUGHT LIKE THE DEVIL"
Hall's 2nd Maine Battery — *July 1, 1863, 10:00-11:00 a.m.*

The Second Maine Battery mustered into service at Augusta, Maine, during the winter of 1861-1862 under the command of Captain Davis Tillson of Rockland.[2] Made up of volunteers mostly from Knox County, the battery also included men from seven other counties in Maine. Stationed at Fort Preble in Portland, the battery left for Washington, D.C., on April 2, 1862. Almost immediately Captain Tillson was promoted to major and given another assignment. Captain James Abram Hall of Damariscotta took over command of the battery. Equipped with six new 3-inch ordnance guns, the battery moved across the Potomac River at the end of April, participating in its first engagement at the Battle of Cross Keys (June 8) as part of General James Shields's division. For the rest of 1862 and the first part of 1863, the battery was involved in most of the major battles of the Army of the Potomac (except Antietam), including the Battle of Cedar Mountain (August, 1862), the Battle of Groveton (August, 1862), the 2nd Battle of Bull Run (August, 1862), the Battle of Fredericksburg (December, 1862), and the Battle of Chancellorsville (May, 1863).

At the Battle of Fredericksburg, Captain Hall demonstrated coolness under fire that

Captain James Hall

became legendary in 1st Corps history. In battle opposite Stonewall Jackson's Corps of the Army of Northern Virginia, the 2nd Maine Battery, as part of Gibbon's Division, became involved in an artillery duel during the morning of December 13, 1862, on the Union Army's left flank. Mounted on horseback, Captain Hall sat conversing with a couple of regimental commanders when a Confederate shell hit a nearby caisson, causing considerable damage. Looking annoyed by this interruption, Hall calmly dismounted and went over to one of his guns. After carefully sighting the weapon he gave the command to fire. The shell hit a Rebel ammunition case, killing all of the men and horses nearby. Hall then remounted his horse and continued the conversation to the rousing cheers of the Union line.[3]

Following the disastrous Union defeat at Chancellorsville, the Army of the Potomac was reorganized. Brigadier General Henry Jackson Hunt became chief of all of the Army's artillery. The batteries in each corps of the Army were placed under his command, taking this responsibility away from division commanders. Colonel Charles S. Wainwright of New York became the 1st Corps artillery chief. His command included the 2nd Maine Battery, the 1st New York Light Artillery, Battery L, the 1st Pennsylvania Battery B, the 5th Maine Battery, and the 4th U.S. Battery B.

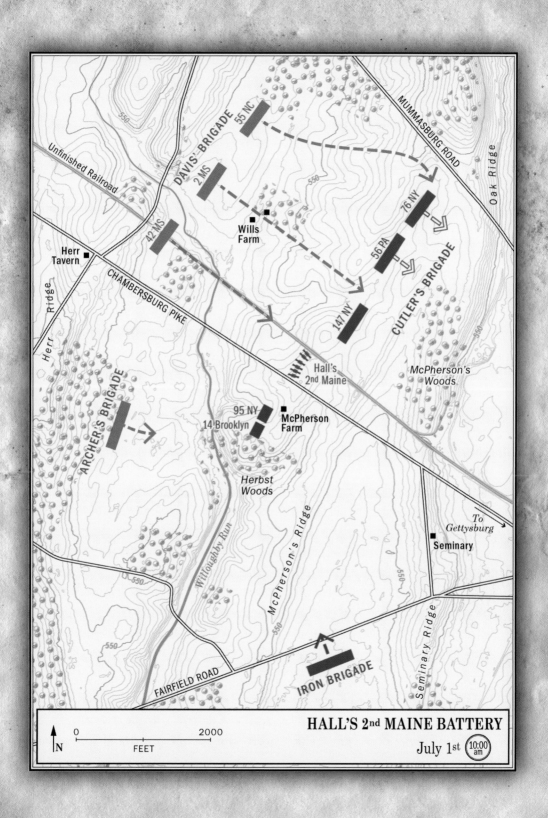

55 NC

DAVIS' BRIGADE

2 MS

MUMMASBURG ROAD

Oak Ridge

Unfinished Railroad

76 NY

42 MS

Wills
Farm

56 PA

CUTLER'S BRIGADE

Herr
Tavern

Herr Ridge

CHAMBERSBURG PIKE

147 NY

McPherson's
Woods

Hall's
2nd Maine

ARCHER'S BRIGADE

95 NY
14 Brooklyn

McPherson
Farm

To
Gettysburg

Seminary

Herbst
Woods

Willoughby Run

McPherson's Ridge

Seminary Ridge

IRON BRIGADE

FAIRFIELD ROAD

HALL'S 2nd MAINE BATTERY

0   2000
FEET

N

July 1st 10:00
am

Leaving their cozy camps near the Rappahannock River in Virginia on June 12, 1863, the 1st Corps crossed the Potomac River into Maryland at Edward's Ferry on June 23. By the evening of June 30, the corps had crossed into Pennsylvania and made camp where the Emmitsburg Road crossed Marsh Creek about five-and-a-half miles south of Gettysburg. Awaking the next day to a leisurely breakfast, the members of the 1st Corps had no idea that in a few hours they would be engaged in a desperate fight.

Artillery at Gettysburg — "It Took a Man's Weight in Lead"

At the Battle of Gettysburg, Maine artillery units used two different types of field cannon. The 2nd Maine Artillery had six 3-inch ordinance guns made of wrought iron. Effective and accurate, the 3-inch gun was the most widely used rifled gun in the army, produced in Pennsylvania at the Phoenix Iron Company. It had a range of 1,830 yards at five degrees of elevation and fired a 9.5-pound shell.

The 5th Maine Battery was equipped with six brass Napoleons (Model 1857, named after French Emperor Napoleon III). The tube was smoothbore rather than rifled, so it was slightly less accurate at a distance but fired a 12-pound shell or ball. It can be recognized for its muzzle-swell (flared front end) and the fact that brass would develop a green patina. It had a range of about 1,600 yards at five degrees of elevation and weighed over 400 pounds more than the three-inch gun, making it much more difficult to move around. In addition, the Napoleon required a charge of two and a half pounds of gun powder compared to the one pound for the 3-inch gun. The 6th Maine Battery serviced four Napoleons during the battle.

Brigadier General Henry J. Hunt, Chief of the Union Artillery, estimated that 32,000 rounds of artillery were fired at Confederate positions at Gettysburg. Since it is generally accepted that artillery caused about ten percent of the casualties during the Civil War, this means that it took about 18.5 rounds to kill or wound one Confederate soldier at the battle.* This compares favorably to the casualty rate per round caused by rifles and pistols at one killed or wounded for every 220 shots (based on estimates that 7 million shots were fired at Gettysburg). By weight, it took about 185 pounds of cannon fire and about 15 pounds of bullets to kill or wound a man — much more than the average weight of a Civil War soldier (about 135 lbs.).

*The open nature of the ground during Pickett's Charge would suggest that a higher percentage of casualties were caused by artillery at Gettysburg. No real study has been done about this. It would take knowing where on the field each casualty occurred in a 1,400-yard-long, mile-wide area. Since most small arms fire did not take effect until the Confederate forces were within 300-400 yards of the Union line on Cemetery Ridge, it could be assumed that most casualties on the field for the first 1,000 yards of the charge were caused by artillery.

As 1st Corps commander Major General John Reynolds rode with his staff toward Gettysburg in the early morning, he was approached by a rider with a message from General John Buford of the Cavalry Corps. Buford reported that the enemy was advancing on the Cashtown Road (Chambersburg Pike) east toward Gettysburg and that his brigade was heavily engaged. Reynolds immediately sent word back to General James Wadsworth, commander of the 1st Division of the 1st Corps to close up the division and march with haste to Gettysburg. In accordance with the marching orders of the day, Hall's 2nd Maine Battery marched with the 1st Division, thus becoming the first Maine unit to be involved in the fighting at Gettysburg. Due to a shortage of men to service the guns, thirty-eight infantrymen from the 16th Maine regiment were attached to the battery.

As Wadsworth's men passed the Codori farm on the Emmitsburg Road just south of Gettysburg, he received orders to bypass the town to the west. Coming onto the scene of the battle at about 10:00 a.m., the men of the 1st Division observed the terrain and the situation. The area west of Gettysburg is dominated by several ridges that run generally from northeast to southwest. About 1,200 yards away lay Herr's Ridge. Though not much more than eighty feet above the surrounding fields, Herr's Ridge was dissected by the Chambersburg Pike. Here the twenty guns of Confederate Colonel William Pegram were posted, engaging in an artillery duel with the Union cavalry's six guns under the command of 1st Lieutenant John Calef.[4] Formed into lines of battle and advancing on either side of the pike were the 7,600 men of Archer's Brigade and Davis's Brigade of Confederate General Henry Heth's division of Hill's 3rd Corps.

They were headed east toward a second rise known as McPherson's Ridge, named after the farm located at the site. About forty feet lower in elevation than Herr's Ridge, McPherson's Ridge was occupied at the moment by General Buford's cavalrymen. Another 650 yards further east was a third ridge line known as

HALL'S BATTERY ON THE FIRST DAY RESISTING THE CONFEDERATE ADVANCE ON THE CHAMBERSBURG ROAD.

Seminary Ridge, named after the Lutheran Theological Seminary that stood there just south of the Chambersburg Pike. North of the Pike, Seminary Ridge became Oak Ridge as it stretched north toward the dominant feature of the battlefield on the first day, Oak Hill.

As Captain Hall on horseback moved to the Chambersburg Pike to survey the situation, he found himself in the company of his commanding generals.

> General Reynolds and Wadsworth, were both at my side . . . and the former extremely anxious, saying to General Wadsworth in the exact following language, "General, move a strong infantry force to Hall's right for he is my defender until I can get the troops now coming up in line. He then said to me, "I desire you to damage the [Confederate] artillery to the greatest possible extent, and keep their fire from our infantry until they are deployed, when I will retire you somewhat, as you are too far advanced for the general line."[5]

As General Lysander Cutler's brigade of Wadsworth's 1st division, led by the 76th New York, the 56th Pennsylvania, and the 147th New York began to cross north of the Chambersburg Pike to form a line, Captain Hall and the 2nd Maine Battery, in a hurry to relieve Calef's battery, cut in front of the 147th New York, causing that regiment to delay its deployment. There across the pike from the McPherson barn, the 2nd Maine Battery deployed its six guns. Across the road to the south, the rest of Cutler's Brigade, the 19th New York and the 14th Brooklyn (84th New York) fell into line to relieve Buford's exhausted cavalrymen.

Captain Hall noted that his battery's first six shots forced the Confederate artillery to move its guns under better cover. However, he did not notice a deep unfinished railroad cut about a hundred yards to the north, running parallel to the Chambersburg Pike. Suddenly Lieutenant Benjamin F. Carr, of Thomaston, reported that the enemy was approaching the right gun of the Battery. These Confederates were members of the 42nd Mississippi regiment of Davis's brigade. With great coolness, Lieutenant William N. Ulmer of Rockland, anticipating an order from Captain Hall, turned the right two guns toward the Mississippians and loaded them with double canister. This fire forced the Mississippians back into the railroad cut, but Confederate skirmishers used the cover of the cut to pick off the artillerists and horses, one by one.

Captain Hall then ordered Lt. Ulmer to take his two guns and retire 300 yards to the rear to enfilade the railroad cut, but Ulmer only barely managed to get his guns to safety, dragging one gun by hand as all of its horses had been shot. It was then that Hall discovered that the entire right flank of Cutler's brigade was retiring, being pressed by the 2nd Mississippi and 55th North Carolina regiments. Knowing that if the field was too hot for infantry then it was certainly too hot for artillery, Hall noted,

> I determined to get the other four guns away if possible and [went]
> to the limbers . . . [and] ordered them to 'reverse' where they were . . .
> Under cover of the smoke I had the guns taken down the slope by hand
> to limber and limbered up, and started for Seminary Ridge. From where
> we limbered up to the point of going into the Cashtown Road, it was
> hellish. The scattering of Rebels along the R.R. cut that had been firing
> upon me . . . rushed forward and fired as rapidly as they could.[6]

The battery was only able to retreat through the field between the railroad cut and the Chambersburg Pike as the road was being covered by Pegram's Confederate artillery. Thinking only to save the guns or die in the attempt, the Maine men had to pause at a low fence in the field which allowed only one gun to pass at a time. At this point Captain Hall was unhorsed. In a letter to Maine's Adjutant General written on July 11, 1863, Hall described the scene;

> [W]e were obliged to drag two guns off by hand. The boys fought
> like the D---l, never better. You may judge when I tell you that many of
> our horses were not shot but bayoneted that it was a close and desperate
> struggle for our guns . . . I have seen hard fighting before, and been badly
> smashed up, but I never saw a battery taken from the field and its guns
> saved in so bad a state as the Old Second came off that day.[7]

One of the four guns was hit by a solid shot and lost a wheel, so Captain Hall was forced to abandon it, temporarily. Retiring finally to Seminary Ridge, Hall in high temper complained, mistakenly it later turned out, to General Wadsworth about the cowardly retreat of the 147th New York, which forced him to abandon his position. Wadsworth denied Hall's request to return to the field to recover his lost gun, instead telling him to "get your guns back to some point to cover the retiring of these troops." Hall replied, "This, General is that place right here in the road." However, Wadsworth insisted, "Oh no, go beyond the town for we cannot hold this line."[8]

Meanwhile, Wadsworth's second brigade, known as the "Iron Brigade," led by Brigadier General Solomon Meredith, had pushed back Archer's regiments, capturing General Archer himself and hundreds of his men. Meredith sent his reserve regiment, the 6th Wisconsin to the railroad cut in combination with the 9th New York and the 14th Brooklyn. There they caught Davis's Brigade of Mississippians and North Carolinians in a deep section of the cut, firing down and forcing them to retreat or surrender.

This completed the morning's activities, leading to a two-hour lull in the fighting. At this time Captain Hall was able to recover his lost gun, after being informed by

Colonel Wainwright that it still lay on the field, and moved the 2nd Maine Battery back through the town of Gettysburg to Cemetery Hill.[9] For the 45 minutes to an hour that the 2nd Maine Battery was engaged it had performed admirably, disabling several enemy guns and repulsing an infantry charge. Eighteen of Hall's men had been wounded and two killed, twenty-eight horses had been killed.

In 1889 Captain Hall reported in Maine at Gettysburg,

> If I should be asked if I could again take the Second Maine Battery as it was July 1, 1863, into action, do what we then did, and get away with so little loss, I should answer "I do not think I could." If repeated a thousand times I would have no hope of once being so highly favored as we were then . . . another company, in the same position and equally as well commanded, might have been destroyed, with no one at fault. I am sure that no mistakes were made by my officers and men, not one. Every man did his full duty and far more.[10]

Meanwhile, General John Reynolds had been killed by a Confederate sniper, and command of the 1st Corps fell to General Abner Doubleday of the 3rd Brigade. Doubleday, wishing to follow Reynolds' general plan, returned the 1st Division to the McPherson's Ridge line. Command of the army on the field fell to Major General Oliver Otis Howard, of Leeds, Maine, who had arrived with the 11th Corps, which was soon posted north of the town. General Howard quickly realized that Cemetery Hill was the key position on the battlefield and began creating a defensive line as a reserve at that location to await further developments. They would be coming soon enough.

"BOYS, YOU KNOW WHAT THAT MEANS"
16th Maine Regiment — *July 1, 1863, 4:00-4:30 p.m.*

In May of 1862 the War Department issued a call for 50,000 troops for three years service, which was expanded to 300,000 troops following the retreat of McClellan's Army of the Potomac after the Seven Days Battles of June that year. In Maine, five new regiments were created in response to the call. On August 13, 1862 the 16th Maine Regiment reported a full complement of 960 enlisted men and 39 officers. Led by Colonel Asa W. Wildes of Skowhegan, the regiment was made up of men from every corner of the State of Maine, from York County in the south to Aroostook County in the north. The regiment started for Washington, D.C., by train on August 19, arriving two days later. It then encamped for the purpose of being drilled by officers and sergeants of the 14th Massachusetts, a veteran unit.

In September, the regiment marched toward Sharpsburg, Maryland but did not participate in the Battle of Antietam. Unfortunately, as they went into camp the men had no tents, knapsacks, or overcoats. These items did not arrive from storage in Washington, D.C., until late November. Having only blankets to keep themselves warm for two months, the men of the 16th Maine took to wearing them around their shoulders. The soldiers in other regiments began derisively calling them the "Blanket Brigade." Many men in the regiment were lost to exposure and sickness during this time, including the regimental commander, Colonel Wildes, who was granted a medical leave.

By December, at the Battle of Fredericksburg, the regiment was down to just over 400 men, now commanded by Lieutenant Colonel Charles W. Tilden of Castine.[11] At Fredericksburg, the regiment went into action for the first time as the only Maine unit in the 1st Corps. Charging the embankment of the Richmond, Fredericksburg and Potomac railroad line, which Confederates were using as a breastwork, the 16th Maine men captured over 200 rebel soldiers during some intense hand-to-hand combat. Forced to retire reluctantly without support, the regiment suffered casualties numbering more than half its strength during its valiant charge. It was the only breakthrough of the Confederate line by Union troops in the entire battle. The term "Blanket Brigade" was never used again.

Lieutenant Colonel Charles W. Tilden

Not seriously engaged at the Battle of Chancellorsville, the regiment mustered 281 men and 32 officers as they left camp near White Oak Church in Virginia on June 12, 1863 as part of General Gabriel Paul's 1st Brigade of General John Robinson's 2nd Division of the 1st Corp. From there the regiment completed several forced marches, suffering with heat and exhaustion just as all of the other regiments in the army did, most recalling the experience as the hardest march of the war. By June 29, the regiment had reached Emmitsburg. The following day saw a brief march to Marsh Run a few miles short of Gettysburg, where the men enjoyed a much needed rest during the day and night.

Just prior to noon on July 1, 1863, General Robinson's Division arrived at Gettysburg, taking position on Seminary Ridge. The men in Paul's Brigade were ordered to fortify the position with breastworks and trenches to prepare the ridge as a defensive line. However, the situation on the battlefield had changed. Confederate General Ewell's 2nd Corps, hearing the sounds of battle, stopped its march towards Cashtown, instead taking the Mummasburg, Carlisle, and Harrisburg Roads east and south toward Gettysburg, arriving at Oak Hill in the early afternoon. Led by Major General Robert E. Rodes's Division, the Confederate forces found themselves facing the right flank of the Union line on Oak and McPherson's Ridges (General Baxter's 2nd Brigade of Robinson's Division and Cutler's 2nd Brigade of Wadsworth's Division) and the left flank of the 11th Corps (Colonel George Von Amsberg's 1st Brigade of Schimmelfennig's Division).

Here General Ewell ordered Rodes's Division to attack down the Mummasburg Road toward Baxter's and Cutler's positions.[12] Due to some poor leadership and coordination in O'Neal's Alabama brigade and Iverson's North Carolina brigade (Iverson did not even take part in this charge), the Confederate forces were thrown back with heavy losses. However, Baxter's Brigade had also suffered casualties and a call for reinforcements was made as the Confederate lines reformed.

Between 1:00-1:30 p.m., Paul's Brigade, including the 16th Maine, began moving north on Seminary Ridge toward the position of Baxter and his men. The captain of Company K, Stephen C. Whitehouse, of Newcastle, turned to the adjutant of the regiment, Major Abner R. Small of Waterville, at this moment, "Goodbye, Adjutant, this is my last fight."[13] Crossing the Chambersburg Pike at the double quick onto Oak Ridge, the regiment faced west and quickly came under fire from a Confederate Battery posted on Oak Hill. Colonel Tilden had his horse shot from under him as the Maine men fought on this line for about two and a half hours, at one point participating in a bayonet charge to clear the area in front of the line of Confederates.

During this phase of the battle a couple of amusing incidents occurred. Second Lieutenant Isaac H. Thompson of Anson noticed a soldier not of the regiment standing about fifteen paces behind the line firing at the rebels. Not wanting his men to be hit from the rear by rifle fire, Thompson went to the man, knocked him down and then raised him up by the collar and kicked him to the rear "much to the merriment and satisfaction of the men, who didn't care to be shot in the back."[14] As the fighting became more intense and casualties in the 16th Maine increased, 1st Lieutenant George A. Deering of Saco sheathed his sword, picked up a musket from a fallen comrade, and joined the ranks in the front line. However, as an officer, it was not really his place to be a rifleman. In nervous excitement he would, every once in a while, forget to return his rammer after loading. . . "hence would send it over to the enemy . . . the peculiar swishing noise made by the rammer, as it hurried through the wood was laughable to the boys, and must have been a holy terror to the rebels."[15]

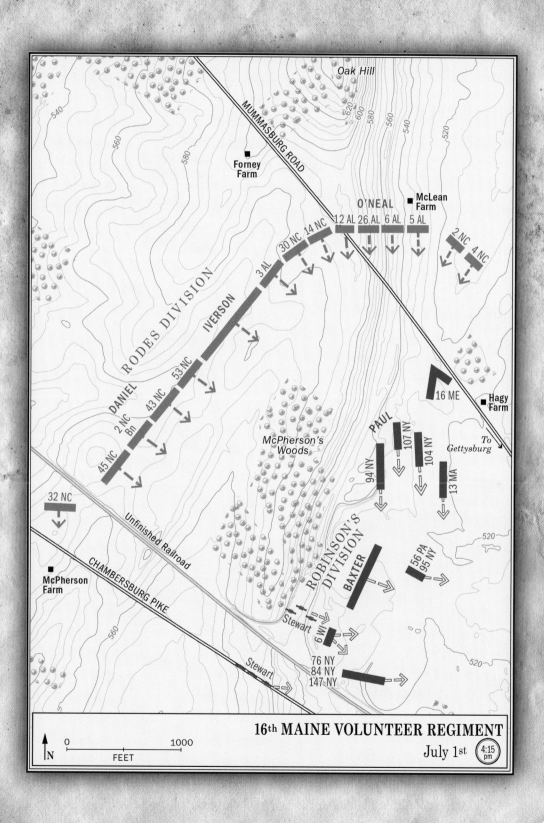

Oak Hill

MUMMASBURG ROAD

Forney
Farm

O'NEAL

McLean
Farm

12 AL 26 AL 6 AL 5 AL

2 NC 4 NC

30 NC 14 NC

3 AL

RODES DIVISION

IVERSON

DANIEL

53 NC

43 NC

2 NC
Bn

45 NC

16 ME

Hagy
Farm

PAUL

107 NY

104 NY

To
Gettysburg

94 NY

13 MA

McPherson's
Woods

32 NC

Unfinished Railroad

ROBINSON'S
DIVISION

BAXTER

56 PA
95 NY

520

CHAMBERSBURG PIKE

McPherson
Farm

560

Stewart

6 WI

76 NY
84 NY
147 NY

Stewart

520

16th MAINE VOLUNTEER REGIMENT

July 1st

4:15
pm

N

0   1000

FEET

While the 1st Corps continued to hold its position on the battlefield, things were not going quite so well north of Gettysburg along the 11th Corps line. At about half past three o'clock, the right flank of the 11th Corps (under the command of Brigadier General Francis Barlow) line broke. Barlow himself was seriously wounded and captured (to be replaced in command by Brigadier General Abelbert Ames of Rockland, Maine) as his men streamed in disorder back through the streets of Gettysburg toward Cemetery Hill. This soon had a domino effect on the rest of the 11th Corps which resulted in the exposing of the rear of Paul's First Brigade. Now faced with the possibility of attacks from the west, north, and east, it was time for the brigade to leave. However, if most of the brigade was to be saved, one regiment would have to stay behind to buy time. Adjutant Small recalled the scene:

> General Robinson rode up to Colonel Tilden. "Advance and hold that hill at any cost," was the order of the Division commander. "Boys, you know what that means," shouted Colonel Tilden. It meant the saving of the rest of the division. It meant death to many, and a captivity worse than death to the survivors of that little band of already exhausted troops, forced by an imperative order to the foot of a sacrificial alter. There was no thought of wavering, but with compressed lips and tense nerves these manly boys silently obeyed their loved commander."

As the men of the regiment advanced they took position behind a stone wall and broke half of the line to the right in an inverted V along the Mummasburg Road. At the apex of the line stood the regiment's color bearers — Sergeant William F. Mower of Greene held the national flag and Corporal Sampson A. Thomas of Turner held the state flag. Although conspicuous targets, they suffered no wounds during this last desperate fight.

Every moment was precious to the retiring division, more than precious to the troops going into position on Cemetery Hill. The deep, hoarse growl of the battle storm grew into a lion-like roar. The rebels fired upon us from all sides, from behind the wall, from the fences, from the Mummasburg Road. They swarmed down upon us, they engulfed us and swept away the last semblance of organization which marked us as a separate command. To fight longer was useless, was wicked. For this little battalion of heroes, hemmed in by thousands of rebels, there was no succor, no hope. Summoned to surrender, Colonel Tildon plunged his sword into the ground and broke it short off at the hilt, and directed the destruction of the colors. A rebel officer sprang to seize the flag, when the men, once more and for the last time, closed around the priceless emblems. Eager hands from every direction seized the banners and tore them piece by piece beyond reclaim or recognition, but now to be held doubly dear. Today, all over Maine, can be found in albums and frames and breast-pocket-books gold stars and shreds of silk, cherished mementos of that heroic and awful hour.[16]

At this point it was every man for himself. By the time the regiment reformed at Cemetery Hill on the evening of July 1, only 35 men and four officers answered the roll call of the 275 men who went into battle, that morning.[17]

During the rest of the battle, the 16th Maine, now commanded by Captain Daniel Marston of Phillips, was held in reserve to the rear of the Evergreen Cemetery. Once sent forward to the line on the 2nd of July while moving past General Meade's headquarters, an exploding shell severely wounded 1st Lieutenant Fred Beecher of Gardiner and seven enlisted men. On July 3, the regiment was held in reserve behind the main line as the men watched the repulse of Pickett's Charge.

Many years later, at a banquet held in honor of the 16th Maine in the town of Gardiner, General Joshua Chamberlain rose to respond to a toast. As he closed a remarkable speech, he spoke of the saving of the colors. At this, a man in the audience stood up and pulled a fragment of the flag from his breast pocket, causing the entire audience to lose control of its emotions. "Yes, and through this tumult of cheers and tears," Chamberlain concluded, "I see that you hold them still to your hearts, precious beyond words, radiant with the glory of service and suffering nobly borne; potent to transmit to other souls the power that has made them glorious!"[18]

"A REGULAR FIRE WAS MAINTAINED"
Stevens's 5th Maine Battery — *July 1, 1863, 4:00-8:30 p.m.*

The 5th Maine Battery was mustered into service in December of 1861 under the command of Captain George F. Leppien of Portland. Stationed for a time at Fort Preble, the battery proceeded to Washington, D.C., in early April in 1862. It commenced field operations in May of the same year, attached to the 3rd Corps of Pope's Army of

Brigadier General Rufus Ingalls — The Supplier

Rufus Ingalls was born in Denmark, Maine, in August of 1818 (in fact, since Maine did not become a state until 1820, technically Ingalls was born in Massachusetts). He graduated 32nd in his class at West Point with his friend, Ulysses S. Grant (23rd in the class). He served in New Mexico and California during the Mexican War and then at various western posts, often with Grant.

He became the Chief Quartermaster of the Army of the Potomac in 1862. As such he was responsible for (1) clothing, camp and garrison equipage, (2) transportation by land and water, and (3) regular and contingent supplies for the Army and the department. Ingalls dealt with a staggering list of duties and responsibilities: the care and feeding of mules and horses, the procuring of wagons, boats and pontoons, tents, food, fuel supplies, coffins, hospital supplies, weapons, cannons, ammunition, building materials, warehouses, blacksmith supplies, wages for mechanics and other laborers, etc.

He served in this capacity at the Battle of Gettysburg. Ingalls's greatest achievement during the war was the construction of the huge supply depot at City Point, Virginia. At the height of the Petersburg campaign in the fall and winter of 1864-65, City Point was the busiest port in the United States, over 100,000 men and 65,000 animals were supplied during this campaign from the port.

Following the war, Ingalls was made the Quartermaster General of the Pacific Division, serving mostly in San Francisco (where a street is named after him). In 1882, he became Quartermaster General of the Army. After retirement, he lived in New York until his death in 1893. He is buried at Arlington National Cemetery.

Virginia. Lightly engaged at Rappahannock Station on August 21 and 22, the battery was heavily engaged at the Second Battle of Bull Run on August 30, 1862. During the general retreat from the battlefield, the battery was overrun, four of the battery's six 12-pound Napoleons were captured by rebel soldiers. In addition, four members of the battery were killed and eight were wounded. After the battle, the 5th Maine Battery was ordered back to Washington, D.C., to be refitted and thus missed going into action during the Battle of Antietam.

On the afternoon of December 13, 1862, the battery took part with other batteries in a brisk cannon duel with Confederate guns during the Battle of Fredericksburg. The rebel guns were silenced in about twenty minutes. In his official report on the battle, the Artillery Chief in Birney's Division, George Randolph noted, "The batteries, of Captains Cooper and Leppien, on my left, did good service. The practice of the 5th Maine (Captain Leppien) attracted my special notice and admiration."[19] The battery maintained its position during the night but was withdrawn the following day.

At the Battle of Chancellorsville in May of 1863, the battery experienced "the most galling and destructive fire" of the war. Stationed in an open field to the right of the Chancellor House, the enemy batteries soon found the exact range. The location of the field "furnished not the slightest protection and our men and horses began to fall before the battery was even in position," according to then Lieutenant Greenlief Stevens of Augusta.[20] Captain Leppien was hit while on horseback by an exploding shell above his ankle, nearly taking the foot off.[21] Lieutenant Stevens was then knocked over by a shell that tore away the clothing on one side of his body, yet only caused a slight flesh wound. Lieutenant Adelbert B. Twitchell of Bethel took command of the battery, but was then wounded himself. With its three

Lieutenant Greenlief Stevens

ranking officers down, Lieutenant Edmund Kirby of the 1st U. S. Battery was ordered by General Couch to take command of the battery. However, almost as soon as he arrived a cannon shot took off one of the fore legs of his horse. Calling for a pistol, he shot the horse but was immediately mortally wounded by another shot. It was then that Corporal James LeBroke of Lewiston finally got permission to remove the guns from the field.

During this brief engagement, the battery lost six men and forty-three horses, and twenty-two men (including the three officers) were wounded. Retreating back over the Rappahannock River, the battery went into camp near White Oak Church and refitted. To make up the losses at Chancellorsville and earlier battles, fifty-three men were detached from the 83rd and 94th New York regiments. By the time the Battle of Gettysburg opened, these men had been thoroughly drilled and disciplined in the artillery arts.

As the battery, with its six brass 12-pound Napoleons, moved on the long march toward Gettysburg in June of 1863, Harvard-educated Captain Greenlief T. Stevens now commanded 83 Maine men plus the New Yorkers for a total of 136 present for duty. Lieutenants Edward N. Whittier and Charles O. Hunt, both from Gorham, were the other commissioned officers. As it was the custom in the artillery during the war to name the battery after its commander, the battery was now known as "Stevens's Battery."

The battery reached the outskirts of Gettysburg sometime between 10:00-11:00 a.m. on July 1. Arriving on Seminary Ridge, Captain Stevens received an order from Colonel Wainwright, Chief of Artillery, to place his battery about 200 yards south of the Theological Seminary. There the Maine men waited during a lull in the fighting. At

Brigadier General Seth Williams — The Nicest Man in the Army

Seth Williams was born in Augusta, Maine, on March 22, 1822. He graduated 23rd in the Class of 1842 from the West Point Military Academy, one spot above classmate Abner Doubleday (24th) and thirty-one spots above James Longstreet (54th). He was cited for gallant and meritorious conduct during the Mexican War.

A friend of General George McClellan (he was a groomsman at McClellan's wedding), he became the Assistant Adjutant-General of the Army of the Potomac, responsible for the routine drafting of orders, correspondence, and reports. He served in that capacity until becoming the Inspector General on General Grant's staff in 1864. He carried Grant's message recommending surrender to Confederate lines. Both he and Rufus Ingalls (also of Maine) were in the room when General Robert E. Lee surrendered at Appomattox in April of 1865. Brevetted a Major General of Volunteers at the end of the war, Williams died one day after his 44th birthday in 1866 of a brain fever. He is buried in Augusta's Forest Grove Cemetery. Fort Williams (now Fort Williams Park), in Cape Elizabeth, is named for him.

However impressive his service, Williams was known in the Army as a nice man. Officers would often, at the end of the day, gather at his tent for company.

"General Williams was simple in manner, courteous in intercourse, constant in friendship, honest in his convictions, and tolerant of adverse opinion. His personal magnetism, inextinguishable cheerfulness, genial nature, and almost feminine gentleness endeared him to all who came within the sunshine of his presence. He never forgot the little amenities of life; his politeness was proverbial, his patience was inexhaustible, and it was his highest gratification to devote himself to the pleasures of others. Hence it was that his unselfishness, modest, sincere sympathy, and steadfast affection made him the loved companion of young and old of both sexes. Yet, with all this light-hearted nature and avoidance of the asperities of life, he was a manly man, a firm patriot, and a brave soldier, who never neglected his fealty to a friend nor a duty to his country."[*]

*Biographical Register of the Officers and Graduates at West Point, Volume 2 by George W. Cullum (New York: 1891), page 132.

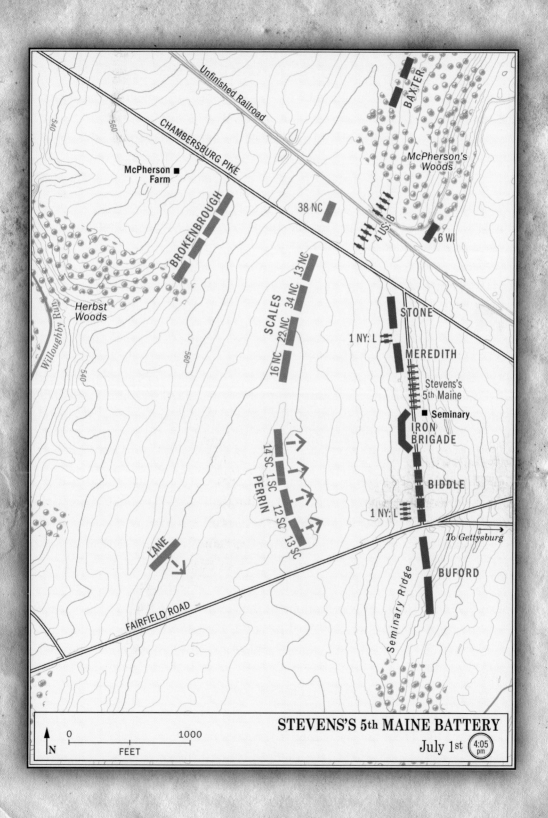

Unfinished Railroad

BAXTER

McPherson's
Woods

CHAMBERSBURG PIKE

McPherson
Farm

BROKENBROUGH

38 NC

4 US: B

6 WI

Herbst
Woods

SCALES

13 NC

34 NC

22 NC

STONE

16 NC

1 NY: L

MEREDITH

Stevens's
5th Maine

Seminary

IRON
BRIGADE

Willoughby Run

14 SC

1 SC

PERRIN

12 SC

BIDDLE

13 SC

1 NY: L

LANE

To Gettysburg

Seminary Ridge

BUFORD

FAIRFIELD ROAD

STEVENS'S 5th MAINE BATTERY

July 1st 4:05 pm

0   1000
FEET

N

about 1:00 p.m., the battery was moved to a position on the ridge almost directly next to the Seminary building, in a line of twelve guns which included the four guns of Cooper's 1st Pennsylvania, Battery B, and two guns of the 1st New York, Battery L. These guns opened fire immediately with both spherical case and shell at Confederate positions near McPherson's Ridge.

Confederate General Heth's two brigades, Pettigrew's and Brockenbrough's, had finally pushed the black-hatted Iron Brigade off McPherson's Ridge but did not advance further, having no orders to follow up the victory (General Heth had been hit in the head by a spent, bullet that nevertheless cracked his skull and rendered him senseless for much of the rest of the battle). Pettigrew's and Brockenbrough's brigades were also spent, so they gave way to Confederate Major General Dorsey Pender's fresh three brigades. At this point, on Seminary Ridge a German staff officer sent by General Otis O. Howard, acting commander on the field, approached General Wainwright with an order to hold Cemetery Hill to the last extremity. Due to the man's thick accent, Wainwright thought he said Seminary Hill as he looked to the defense of his position.

As Pender's Division approached the Seminary Hill line at about 4:00 p.m., the men of Stevens's Battery began firing canister charges and then double canister that barely cleared the heads of the 150th Pennsylvania and 7th Wisconsin formed almost directly in front of them. The shot-gun like effect of the canister stopped Pender's men cold, only one flag bearer reaching the Union line. However, outnumbered about five to one, the blue-clad infantry began to waiver as Pender's second line advanced. With a yell, the men from North and South Carolina charged and the Union line collapsed.[22]

General Wadsworth, in charge of the infantry at this spot, found Captain Stevens and ordered him to retreat to the rear. However, Colonel Wainwright appeared and countermanded that order, perhaps remembering Howard's order to hold to the end. But, a quick look at the situation forced him to reconsider. Retreating as calmly but as quickly as possible, the battery experienced some difficulty descending the eastern slope of Seminary Ridge. A wheel of one of the guns came off. "The team was halted, the gun raised by cannoneers and wheel replaced. Captain Stevens springing from his horse and seizing the gunner's pinchers, inserted the handle for a linch-pin, and the gun was saved."[23]

Struggling through the streets of Gettysburg, crowded with the fleeing men of both the 1st and 11th Corps, the 5th Maine Battery finally made it to the rendezvous point at Cemetery Hill. There they were met at the gates of the cemetery by Major General Winfield Scott Hancock, who had been sent by General Meade to take command of the forces on the field.[24] As the battery came up Hancock called for the captain of "that brass battery." Captain Stevens heard what he said and approached Hancock, who ordered Stevens to "take (his) battery on to that hill," pointing to Culp's Hill, and "stop the enemy from coming up that ravine." "By whose order?" was the inquiry. "General Hancock's," was the reply.[25]

Moving to a knoll on the western slope of Culp's Hill, the 5th Maine Battery found itself in an excellent position. From this spot, a battery could control the entire easterly slope of Cemetery Hill and the ravine that separated the two spots. However, it also found itself in place without any infantry support. General Henry Hunt, chief of all artillery in the Union Army, suddenly appeared and told Captain Stevens. "I don't like the look of this; send some of your men and tear gaps in the fences between here and the Baltimore Pike, and on the opposite side of the pike, so that you can reach the high land beyond in case you are driven out."[26]

But General Hancock had not forgotten his six guns on Culp's Hill. He soon ordered General Abner Doubleday to send the remainder of General Wadsworth's Division of the 1st Corps over as support. Still, the line was very thin and the men of the 5th Maine Battery had to remain vigilant. Lieutenant Whittier in his after action report noted, "A regular fire was maintained until dark to prevent the enemy occupying the ground in front."[27] Finally, close to 6:00 p.m., units from Major General Slocum's 12th Corps, that had been marching slowly much of the day, arrived on the scene, taking positions on the left flank. During the night, earthworks were constructed to protect the battery and finally the men fell to the earth exhausted. "Thus passed one of our days and nights on this battlefield destined to become the Waterloo of the western world."[28] The battery had suffered two men killed, six men wounded and five men taken prisoner.

NOTES

1. Captain Tillson had attended the Military Academy at West Point but was forced to resign before graduating due to a foot injury, which led to amputation. He eventually rose to the rank of Major General of Volunteers during the Civil War, serving mostly in Tennessee. Following the war, Tillson established a granite quarry on Hurricane Island in Penobscot Bay. Granite from Tillson's quarry is one of the major components of the Washington Monument in the nation's capital.

2. Small, Abner R., *The Road to Richmond: The Civil War Letters of Major Abner R. Small of the 16th Maine Volunteers* (University of California Press, 1939), page 65.

3. "Willie" Pegram was General A. P. Hill's favorite artilleryman. A young 22 years old, Pegram was fearless in battle but had a physical defect that one would not expect of a leader of artillery . . . he was extremely nearsighted and always wore his gold-rimmed glasses into battle. He was killed at the Battle of Five Forks in April of 1865, just eight days before the end of the war.

4. James Hall to John Bachelder, February 27, 1867, Bacheldor Papers, (I): page 306.

5. James Hall to John Bachelder, December 29, 1869, Bacheldor Papers, (I): pages 386-387.

6. Letter of James A. Hall to John L. Hodsdon, July 11, 1863, Maine Adjutant General's Records, 2nd Maine Battery file.

7. *The War of the Rebellion: a Compilation of the Official Records of the Union and Confederate Armies*, Government Printing Office, Volume 27 (1): pages 359-360 (hereafter known as OR). Disregarding Wadsworth's orders, Hall did send six men to recover the lost gun. They all were either captured or killed.

8. Posted there on what is now the eastern slope of the National Cemetery, Hall's 2nd Maine Battery participated in repelling a Confederate charge during the evening of July 2, 1863. During the entire battle, Captain Hall reported that the battery fired 635 rounds of ammunition.

9. *Maine at Gettysburg: Report of Maine Commissioners Prepared by the Executive Committee*, (1898), page 19.

10. Tilden already had a great deal of experience during the war, having served as 1st Lieutenant and then Captain of Company B of the 2nd Maine regiment. At the First Battle of Bull Run the 2nd Maine regiment suffered 47 killed or wounded, as it was the last regiment to leave the battlefield. Following the Battle of Chancellorsville, Tilden contracted dysentery and malaria and was forced to leave the regiment for a while. He returned to the 16th Maine just prior to the Battle of Gettysburg and served to the end of the war, occasionally plagued by recurring bouts of his illness.

11. While General Henry Heth has taken much of the blame for initiating the Battle of Gettysburg while under orders to not bring on an engagement, the real culprit was General Ewell, who pushed his corps forward down Oak Hill.

12. Small, Abner R., *The Sixteenth Maine Regiment in the War of the Rebellion*, (Portland, Maine: 1886), page 117. Major Small near saw Captain Whitehouse again.

13. Ibid., page 119.

14. Ibid.

15. *Maine at Gettysburg*, pages 46-47.

16. Ibid., page 47. The men of the 16th Maine hide the remnants of the colors under their clothing, many eventually making their way back to Maine. The Maine State Museum at Augusta, Maine has several pieces in its collection.

17. As in all casualty reports and body counts, there is some confusion concerning the final tally sheet of the 16th Maine at Gettysburg. Its marker on the

Mummasburg Road lists 11 killed, 62 wounded, and 159 captured for a total of 222 casualties, its main monument on Doubleday Avenue lists one additional wounded for a total of 223 casualties, while the revised casualty report lists 21 killed, 53 wounded, 97 captured, and 5 missing for a total of 176 casualties. Whichever is correct, this means that at least 42 and as many as 99 men eventually made their way back to the regiment, avoiding both bullets and capture. One story in particular is amusing, demonstrating a little Yankee ingenuity. Private Benjamin F. Worth of Vassalboro was captured as a member of Company E during the 16th Regiment's stand on Oak Ridge. Sent by his captors to pick up rifles on the battlefield on July 2, Benny, as he was known in the regiment, made his way to a Confederate field hospital, where he found some bloody bandages. Wrapping the bandages around an imaginary wound on his ankle, he was left behind by the retreating Confederates and made his way back to the 16th Maine on July 4.

Taken prisoner, Colonel Tilden was sent to the infamous Libby Prison in Richmond, Virginia. He was kept there until he took part in one of the most daring prison escapes in history. On February 9, 1864, 109 captives used a tunnel to break out of the prison. Fifty-nine of them made it back to Union lines, including Colonel Tilden. He returned to the 16th Maine in time for the spring campaign and marched with the regiment to Appomattox at the end of the war. A side note — Libby Prison was originally a warehouse leased in Richmond by Captain Luther Libby . . . a native of Maine.

18. *Maine at Gettysburg,* page 66.

19. *OR,* Volume 21, page 365.

20. *Maine at Gettysburg,* page 107.

21. The foot was amputated but Captain Leppien died twenty days later in Washington, D.C. He is buried in Laurel Hill Cemetery in Philadelphia, the city of his birth.

22. At this point, Lieutenant Charles Oliver Hunt was wounded in the upper part of his right thigh. Hunt had been in Gettysburg before. Ironically, his sister, Mary, had married Thomas D. Carson, the cashier of the only bank in Gettysburg. In May of 1862, while on leave, Hunt had visited his sister but became sick. He was treated during his illness by Dr. Charles Hamme. So now, a year later, Lt. Hunt got permission to ride to his sister's home to get treatment for his wound. Arriving at her home, he found no one there but on a hunch went to the bank building. There he found his sister and eighteen other women and children (and two dogs) huddled for protection in the bank vault (the contents of the vault having been sent to Philadelphia prior to the battle). Finding Dr. Hamme, it was discovered that Hunt's pistol butt had slowed the bullet but a piece of it had entered the

wound making it look worse than it was. The next day, July 2, while resting in his sister's house, two Confederate officers entered the house looking for any Union soldiers. Because he was wounded, they decided to leave him but told him they would be back the next day to take him prisoner. They never came back. After the war, Hunt went to medical college and eventually became the Superintendent of Maine General Hospital in Portland. His diary from the war can be viewed at the Maine State Archives in Augusta.

23. *Maine at Gettysburg,* page 86.

24. Needless to say, the meeting between Hancock, who arrived on the field at about 4 p.m., and Howard on Cemetery Hill was awkward. To summarize, Hancock was brusque in manner, with an order to take charge from General Meade in his pocket. Howard was deeply offended that someone he outranked had been given command of the field, but he was gracious. The men agreed to work together to save the valuable piece of ground they stood on.

25. Ibid., page 89.

26. Ibid., pages 89-90.

27. From Lt. Edward N Whittier's letter to Maine Adjutant General A. L. Hodsdon, August 2, 1863, Maine State Archives.

28. Ibid., page 91.

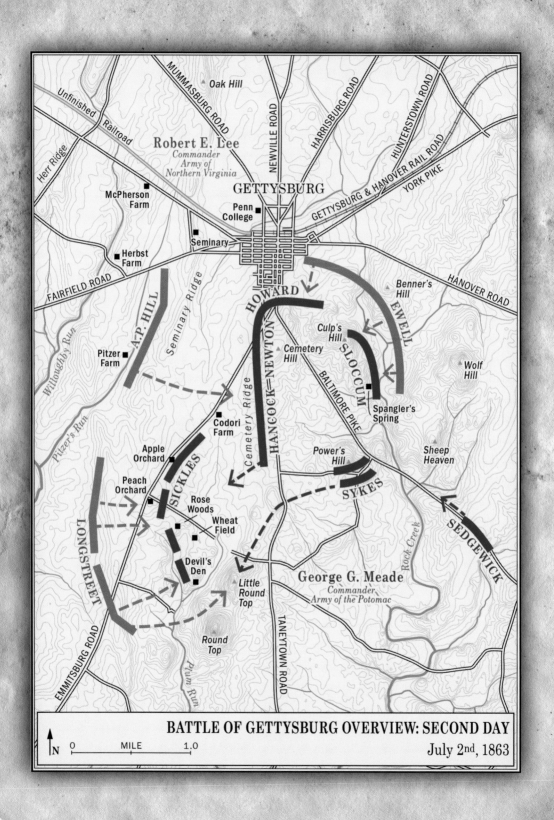

BATTLE OF GETTYSBURG OVERVIEW: SECOND DAY

July 2nd, 1863

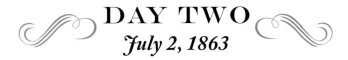

DAY TWO
July 2, 1863
LONGSTREET ATTACKS

As the second day of the battle at Gettysburg began, Dr. Jacobs at Pennsylvania College recorded a morning much like the day before, with a slight breeze from the south, an overcast sky, and a temperature of 74 degrees. By 2:00 p.m., the temperature would rise to the low to mid 80s. General Robert E. Lee arose early before sunrise at 4:37 a.m. after only two or three hours of sleep to survey the battlefield.

General Robert E. Lee

All of Ewell's 2nd Corps and Hill's 3rd Corps were on the field, stretching from the Hanover Road north of Culp's Hill through the town of Gettysburg and west over to Seminary Ridge. These two corps had suffered about 6,500 casualties during the first day's fight. Two fresh divisions of Longstreet's 1st Corps were posted along the Chambersburg Pike. General J.E.B. Stuart's Cavalry was still missing somewhere to the east. General Pickett's division of the 1st Corps was near Chambersburg at least a day's march away to the west guarding supplies, a duty that Stuart's Cavalry should have been performing (had Pickett's men been where they should have been, with the rest of Longstreet's Corps, perhaps the second day at Gettysburg would have turned out differently).

Lee quickly sent out a scout to the south to reconnoiter the left flank of the Union army. Returning about 8:00 a.m., the scout reported that the two large hills to the south were unoccupied. With this information, Lee decided to move Longstreet's Corps to the right in order to move up the Emmitsburg Road and roll up the Federal left flank. Longstreet suggested a move to the south behind the Federal army, placing the Army of Northern Virginia in a defensive position between Meade's army and Washington, D.C., but this plan was rejected. "The enemy is here," Lee remarked to General John B. Hood, one of the division commanders in Longstreet's Corp, "and if we do not whip him, he will whip us."[29]

General Meade had arrived on the battlefield around midnight, only his third day in command of the Army of the Potomac. The situation he found was grim but the ground the army held was excellent for defense. The 1st and 11th Corps were decimated, having suffered together almost 9,000 casualties on July 1. Fortunately, the 2nd Corps, 12th Corps, and 3rd Corps had arrived on the scene with over 30,000 men to shore up the lines on Culp's Hill and Cemetery Ridge. The 5th Corps, with an additional 11,000 men was moving up the Baltimore Pike and would soon arrive on the battlefield to take position as a reserve. The Federal Cavalry Corps was also on or near the battlefield in force under the command of Major General Alfred Pleasonton.

However, Major General Daniel Sickles was not happy about his position on the field. Suspecting a Confederate flanking maneuver, he moved the entire 3rd Corps forward, without orders, from Cemetery Ridge to the Emmitsburg Road near the Sherfy farm peach orchard. Meanwhile, finding that scouting reports were not correct, Longstreet's flanking maneuver was delayed by counter-marching to try to avoid detection. His attack on the Union left flank did not begin until 4:00 p.m. in the late afternoon.

For four hours, Longstreet's men fought in places that have since become legend, the Peach Orchard, Devil's Den, the Wheatfield, and Little Round Top. On each, Maine men held key positions in the Union line, including the 3rd Maine, 4th Maine, 17th Maine, Dow's 6th Maine Battery, the 19th Maine, and the 20th Maine. On Culp's Hill, as General Ewell attempted to take positions on the Union right in support of Longstreet's advance, Stevens's 5th Maine Battery performed heroically.

By the end of the day, the Union army still held the high ground. Confederate forces had come within a whisker of success and made some advances, but failed to crush the Union left flank. General Lee, frustrated by what seemed to be a lack of coordination by his army on the field, then turned his thoughts to a desperate gamble. There would be one more day of battle at Gettysburg.

"QUITE A SPIRITED LITTLE FIGHT"
3rd Maine Regiment — *July 2, 1863, Noon*

The Oxford Dictionary definition of the word "rascal," is missing a line. It should include, "e.g., Major General Daniel E. Sickles." Prior to the war, Sickles had been a politician in New York but was most famous for being the first man in the country to get away with murder by using the temporary insanity plea (having killed his wife's lover, Philip Barton Key, the son of Francis Scott Key of *Star Spangled Banner* fame, in broad daylight on Lafayette Square in Washington, D.C., in 1859). Using his political influence and friendship with General Hooker (a fellow rascal), Sickles had risen to the command of the 3rd Corps, the only corps commander in the Army of the Potomac who had not graduated from the West Point Military Academy.

While surveying the position of his corps on the morning of July 2, Sickles was dissatisfied. His men were placed on the lower slope of Cemetery Ridge down toward Little Round Top. He felt that a better position would be directly to the west about half a mile to high ground on the Emmitsburg Road. In conversation with General Meade that morning he suggested such a move but was told to hold his position where he was. However, Meade did send Artillery Chief General Henry Hunt over to Sickles's corps to see what could be done to extend the line. Hunt suggested that Sickles send out a scouting party west to an area on the other side of the Emmitsburg Road known as Pitzer's Woods to determine if there was any movement there by Confederate troops. So, just prior to noon, General Sickles sent out two regiments of his corps, the renowned 1st U.S. Sharpshooters, under the command of Colonel Hiram Berdan, and the 3rd Maine regiment.

There was probably not a more veteran unit in the Army of the Potomac on that day than the 3rd Maine Regiment. Mustered into service on June 4, 1861, under the command of Colonel Oliver Otis Howard, the regiment was made up of men from Kennebec and Sagadahoc counties (Company A having formerly been a militia unit known as the Bath City Greys). Participating in its first engagement at the First Battle of Bull Run in July of 1861, the regiment suffered 49 casualties. Over the next two years the regiment would go into action at most of the major battles of the Army of the Potomac, including the Peninsula Campaign, Second Bull Run, Antietam, Fredericksburg, and Chancellorsville. At Fredericksburg, the regiment, posted in support of the 2nd Maine Battery, sustaining thirty-two casualties while remaining on the field for fifty hours before being withdrawn. At Chancellorsville, the 3rd Maine, now under the command of Colonel Moses B. Lakeman of Augusta, sustained sixty casualties holding a line of earthworks until May 6, being one of the last regiments in the army to be withdrawn back over the Rappahannock River.

By the time the regiment reached Gettysburg, it was down to 196 men and fourteen officers, serving as part of the 2nd Brigade, 1st Division of the 3rd Corps. Receiving orders to move behind the Sharpshooters to the west, the 3rd Maine had to cover three quarters of a mile over the Emmittsburg Road and then an open field to the thick oak and chestnut trees of Pitzer's Woods. There they found that the Sharpshooters had already engaged with Confederates, in fact three whole regiments of Confederates. Coming up in support, the 3rd Maine engaged in a brief but unequal combat for about twenty-five minutes before the bugle sounded retreat, having suffered forty-eight casualties, including over thirty of the men being captured. Many years later in a newspaper interview the Confederate commander on the field called it "quite a spirited little fight."[30]

Leaving their dead and some of their wounded on the field, the 3rd Maine and the Sharpshooters retreated back to their former line. There the results of the reconnaissance were reported to General Sickles, confirming in his mind, the fact that the Confederates were attempting a flanking maneuver.[31] He immediately, without orders from General

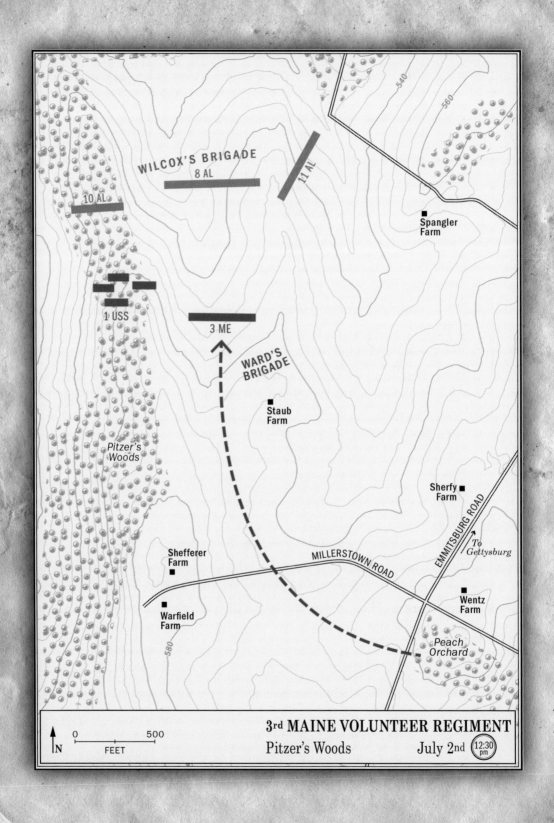

WILCOX'S BRIGADE

8 AL

11 AL

10 AL

1 USS

3 ME

WARD'S
BRIGADE

Pitzer's
Woods

Spangler
Farm

Staub
Farm

Sherfy
Farm

Shefferer
Farm

MILLERSTOWN ROAD

EMMITSBURG ROAD

To
Gettysburg

Wentz
Farm

Warfield
Farm

Peach
Orchard

540

560

580

0   500
FEET

N

3rd MAINE VOLUNTEER REGIMENT
Pitzer's Woods

July 2nd

12:30
pm

Meade, advanced his entire corps to positions on the Emmitsburg Road at Sherfy's Peach Orchard and south to an area known as "Devil's Den."

However, this move created a huge gap between the 2nd Corps on Cemetery Ridge and the 3rd Corps on its right flank and left the two Round Top hills unprotected. When General Meade found out about the move, he rode out to meet General Sickles to explain the precarious position that he now held. Sickles offered to retreat back to his original position but Meade replied that it was too late "the enemy will not let you get away without a fight, and it may begin now at any time."[32] Almost on cue, the Confederate artillery began shelling the 3rd Corps. It was 4:00 p.m. as General Meade rode back to find a way to support Sickles's exposed corps.[33]

"BUT FOR THE SERVICE ON YOUR PART"
Company D, 2nd U. S. Sharpshooters — *July 2, 1863, 4:00-5:30 p.m.*

Hiram C. Berdan was the type of person who always had something going on, often several things at once. Born in New York in 1824 and raised in Michigan, Berdan as a young man trained at Hobart College in Geneva, New York, as a mechanical engineer, soon putting his considerable talents to work inventing all kinds of things. In all, he held over thirty U. S. patents by the time of his death in 1893, including several engines of war, the invention of the collapsible lifeboat, an automated bread maker, a reaper, and a commercial gold amalgamation machine to separate gold from ore. His various inventions made him a very wealthy and famous man, giving him the resources to pursue his one major passion — sport shooting.

By 1861, Berdan had become perhaps the nation's leading competitive marksman, having won numerous shooting matches over the previous fifteen years. As such, at the beginning of the Civil War, he found support in the War Department for another brainchild . . . to search the country for the best marksmen in order to form a corps of riflemen

for service in the Union Army under his command.[34]

A call went out in newspapers across the nation for applicants for this elite regiment. Shooting competitions were soon held in small towns and cities in the northern states, becoming exciting public spectacles. Men trying out for the Sharpshooters were required at a distance of 600 feet (the length of two football fields today) to put ten consecutive shots in a target circle of ten inches in diameter, about the size of a piece of letter copy paper today. The applicants could use their own rifle or choose a rifle. They could stand or kneel at rest while shooting and were allowed to use a telescopic sight or a target globe sight. They could also qualify by making the same ten shots at the same target at 300 feet using open sights while not at rest, known as an "off hand" shot.

By end of 1861, Berdan had selected and enrolled almost 1,000 men, taking command of a ten company regiment composed of the best marksmen from New York, Michigan, Wisconsin, New Hampshire, and Vermont. The Army designated the regiment as the 1st U. S. Sharpshooters. Although Hiram Berdan eventually proved to be a less than able leader of men (he was often found absent during important battles), he was an effective recruiter. The War Department allowed him to raise an additional eight companies at the end of 1861 to form the 2nd U. S. Sharpshooters. These 800 men came from six different states — Company A (Minnesota), Company B (Michigan), Company C (Pennsylvania), Company D (Maine), Company E (Vermont), Company F (New Hampshire), Company G (New Hampshire), and Company H (Vermont).

Berdan had his first regiment outfitted with what he thought was the best weapon of the day, the Model 1859 Sharps rifle, produced by the Sharps Rifle Manufacturing Company in Hartford, Connecticut. Designed by Christian Sharps and patented in 1848, the Sharps rifle had a unique sliding breech-block mechanism, which allowed the user to load cartridges at twice the speed of a muzzle-loading rifle or musket.[35] In addition, instead of forcing the rifleman to fix a percussion cap on the nipple at the rear end of the gun barrel for each shot, the Sharps rifle had a pellet primer system that flipped over the nipple each time the trigger was pulled, thus saving a great deal of time.[36]

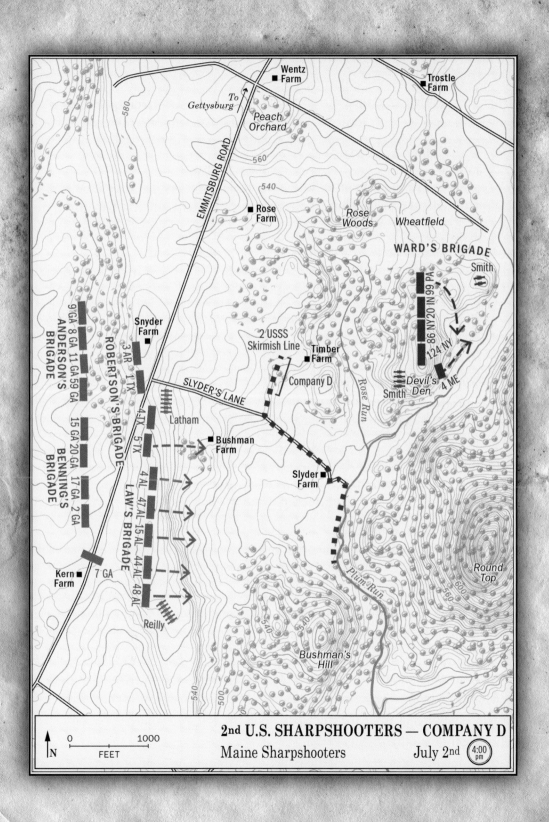

Wentz
Farm

Trostle
Farm

To Gettysburg

Peach Orchard

EMMITSBURG ROAD

Rose Farm

Rose Woods

Wheatfield

WARD'S BRIGADE

Smith

86 NY 20 IN 99 PA

124 NY

9 GA 8 GA 11 GA 59 GA

ANDERSON'S BRIGADE

Snyder Farm

ROBERTSON'S BRIGADE

3 AR 1 TX

2 USSS Skirmish Line

Timber Farm

Company D

Rose Run

Smith

Devil's Den

4 ME

SLYDER'S LANE

4 TX

Latham

15 GA 20 GA

17 GA 2 GA

BENNING'S BRIGADE

5 TX

LAW'S BRIGADE

Bushman Farm

4 AL

47 AL

15 AL

44 AL

48 AL

Slyder Farm

Plum Run

Round Top

Kern Farm

7 GA

Reilly

Bushman's Hill

0   1000

FEET

N

2nd U.S. SHARPSHOOTERS — COMPANY D

Maine Sharpshooters

July 2nd 4:00 pm

For every three shots that a very competent rifleman with a breech loading weapon could fire in a minute, a sharpshooter could fire seven or even eight shots with the Sharps rifle.[37] However, many of the men were allowed to use their own weapons if they preferred as long as they could maintain accuracy and a rate of fire. Some members of the regiment even had specially made long distance rifles with telescopic mounts, such as the .45-caliber British Whitworth rifle, or individually crafted and extremely heavy match or sniper rifles.

Copying the British and other European models, Berdan had his men wear a dark green frock coat with black rubber buttons (to reduce reflection) as an early form of camouflage, rather than the traditional blue uniform of the regular army. They were also issued heavy leather leggings to keep trouser legs from being torn or caught in dense forest growth and a unique hairy cowhide knapsack created by Tiffany's of New York. The sharpshooters called them "hair trunks."

The regiment received the same basic training as other regiments in the Civil War, learning to march, to perform the manual of arms and the formal movements of various close order drills, and to set up camp. However, as a sharpshooter regiment, the men were also trained for three addition duties — sharpshooting, scouting (today known as intelligence gathering), and skirmishing. The first, sharpshooting, came naturally to these men. However, the 19th-century ideal of the battlefield involved heroic man-to-man combat, with armies close enough to "see the whites of their eyes." The idea of long distance killing was abhorrent to many in the ranks. It took a certain amount of cold bloodedness to shoot a man who was 500 to 1,500 feet away. To some, sniping seemed like assassination not war and many were shocked by the casualness that the sharpshooters displayed as they went about their business.

Scouting and skirmishing often were performed at the same time. The sharpshooters were usually posted in advance of the main body of the army or on either flank. Their job was to find where the enemy was, to determine the enemy's strength if practicable, and delay the enemy long enough to warn the main body of an impending attack. At this level, skirmishers followed a set of basic rules much like a choreographed dance. The men worked in teams of four men, two in front and two to the rear, usually posted five to seven paces apart often performing on the run. If retreating, after the front two fired they would retreat behind to back two men who would hold their fire until their partners had reloaded. If advancing, after the front two fired, the rear two would move ahead, again not firing until the others had reloaded.

Sharpshooters were trained to make use of the terrain, to adjust to the situation and to fight independently if necessary. The men of the 1st and 2nd U. S. Sharpshooters were, for the most part, highly intelligent. Many of the enlisted men in these regiments could have been officers in the regular army and volunteer regiments. They were members of an elite unit and they knew it, much like the Special Forces today or the Green Berets of the Vietnam era (there is that color again). This high amount of confidence often made these units difficult to manage. A couple of incidents during the war can be used to illustrate this point.

After muster, Colonel Berdan decided in February of 1862 that the newest regiment, the 2nd U. S. Sharpshooters should be issued the Model 1855 Colt revolving rifle instead of the Sharps rifle. The problem with the Colt was that the cartridges in the revolving cylinder of the rifle were just as likely to fire all at once as soon as the trigger was pulled. Many soldiers considered it to be a dangerous weapon to fire. In his diary, Sergeant James Mero Matthews from Rockland, Maine, serving in Company D, described the scene:

> Great times these. The Co. was taken to Hdqrs. by the orderly to receive the celebrated Colt's Rifles, the gun Col. Berdan, report says, will have a commission on if sold to the government. The roll was called and Orderly Hall was the first to refuse the gun saying "it was not the gun he enlisted for." Col. Post immediately took charge of him, marched him to the 1st Reg guard house, where he was introduced to a pair of steel bracelets and thence turned over to our guard at the guard tent. That started up the spark and every one of the company refused the gun. Col. Post immediately returned and said while standing in the entrance of the tent — "As there are many of Co. D here, I will say as true as there is a God in Heaven, the first man of every company that refuses to take one of these guns will be shot by a regiment of regulars. Now if you wish to save your Orderly" . . . The balance of this very interesting speech was either cut short by the noise in the crowd, or was never uttered. The Col. doubtless takes this method of frightening our company, but he was mistaken in the men. Although many of the men are from the "backwoods" they are not to be frightened by an "owl." Instead of softening the feeling, it increased its temperature to a boiling point and nothing save military discipline could quell it. As soon as all had made NO to the answer as name was called, we were marched to our quarters and put under arrest.[38]

Soon the mini-revolt spread throughout the regiment. While the men were eventually forced to accept the Colts. . . by May of 1862, after applying some political pressure, including an intervention by Maine's very influential Senator, William Pitt Fessenden, the regiment finally got its Sharps rifles.

The second incident occurred not long after the Battle of Gettysburg. Closely following the Army of Northern Virginia during its retreat back into Virginia, the 2nd U. S. Sharpshooters found themselves without rations after a long day of marching. They started shouting, "Hardtack! Hardtack! Hardtack!" clamoring for anything to eat, even that tasteless army cracker. Responding to the shouts, brigade commander General J. H. Hobart Ward rode to the regiment, drawing his pistol, "God damn your souls! I'll give you hardtack! The first man that says hardtack I will put a ball through!"[39] As he turned to ride away the entire regiment yelled, "Hardtack!" General Ward moved to un-holster his pistol to follow through on his deadly warning, only to hear every member of the regiment click the hammer of his rifle to the ready position. The general thought better of the situation and wisely rode on, only later to order the entire regiment on that evening's picket duty.

Both sharpshooter regiments fought in the Peninsular Campaign, the Second Battle of Bull Run, the battles of Antietam, Fredericksburg, and Chancellorsville, and many other smaller engagements. By the first days of June 1863, the hundred men from Maine of Company D, 2nd U.S. Sharpshooters had been reduced to the following thirty-four soldiers:

Although the Battle of Chancellorsville in early May of 1863 had been a resounding Confederate victory, the two sharpshooters regiments had performed admirably. In fact, they had accomplished the amazing feat of capturing the bulk of an entire southern regiment, the 23rd Georgia Infantry. Falling back over the Rappahannock River, the 2nd

Sharpshooter – CoD	Rank	Hometown	Fought in Battle of Gettysburg?
Jacob McClure	Captain	Rockland	Yes
Josiah Gray	First Sergeant	Prentiss	Yes
Steven C. Barker	Sergeant	Island Falls	Yes
Edgar Crockett	Sergeant	Rockland	Yes
James M. Matthews	Sergeant	Rockland	Yes
John E. Wade	Sergeant	Rockland	Yes
Richard Boynton	Corporal	Jefferson	Yes
George H. Coffin	Corporal	Cherryfield	Yes
Luther G. Davis	Corporal	Cherryfield	No, detached pioneer corps
Argyl D. Morse	Corporal	Rockland	Yes
John H. Rounds	Corporal	Portland	Yes
George U. Leighton	Corporal	Jonesport	Yes
John B. Allen	Private	Marshfield	Yes
Albert Bickford	Private	Carratunk Plantation	No, detached ambulance corps
James C. Bradbury	Private	Burlington	Yes
Barzillia D. Bragg	Private	Rockland	Yes
Henry Brown	Private	Rockland	Yes
Oscar Dunbar	Private	Cherryfield	Yes
Stillman M. Emerson	Private	Addison	Yes
John M. Hussey	Private	China	No, teamster
John J. Jameson	Private	Rockland	Yes
Francis W. Ladd	Private	Vienna	Yes
Edward Lindsay	Private	Rockland	Yes
William A. McFarland	Private	Cherryfield	No, detached ambulance corps
Simon McLain	Private	Lowell	Yes
Albion Morey	Private	Machias	Yes
James N. Pendleton	Private	Rockland	Yes
James F. Salley	Private	Madison	Yes
John Sullivan	Private	Addison	Yes
Charles O. Wentworth	Private	Rockland	Yes
Charles S. White	Private	Greenbush	No, detached ambulance corps
John M. Wilson	Private	Rockland	No, teamster
Wilson R. Woodward	Private	Bangor	No, quartermaster
William H. Young	Private	Sidney	Yes

Sharpshooters went back into camp at Stoneman's Station along the Aquia RR line near Falmouth, Virginia. They stayed in camp until June 11, when ordered to march to Rappahannock Station, then continued in the following days through Centerville and Gum Springs, Virginia. The 2nd Sharpshooters regiment crossed the Potomac River into Maryland at Edward's Ferry on June 25. Along the way, on June 23, the regiment was "attacked" by a flock of about thirty sheep, which were soon captured and pressed into service.

As the men marched north towards Taneytown, Maryland, they were pleased to find that the residents of the state were strongly pro-Union. Sergeant Matthews recorded in his diary on June 29:

> We passed through Walkersville & Woodsboro today. It is said we are about 8 miles from Pennsylvania. The citizens flocked to the road to witness the passing of the troops. As we passed through Taneyville [Taneytown} the girls were out. One squad, after we had given them three cheers, endeavored to return the compliment, but all we could hear was a jumbling of voices with cheers for the Sharpshooters etc. As their intentions were good, we passed on. The Union feeling is plainly to be seen in marching through these places. Had biscuit for dinner. Marched about 16 miles.[40]

After a hard and hot march on July 1 the 3rd Corps reached the outskirts of Gettysburg at dusk, posting along the southern end of Cemetery Ridge as the anchor of the Army of the Potomac's left flank. The 169 men of the 2nd U.S. Sharpshooters, under the command of Major Homer Stoughton of Vermont, awoke early at 5:00 a.m. on July 2, but stayed in position for several hours at rest.[41] Sometime in mid-morning the regiment was ordered forward to cover the flank of the corps in a ravine (now known as the "Valley of Death"). The Maine men in Company D held a position near a small stream called Rose Run to the immediate west of Devil's Den.

At around 2:00 p.m., General Sickles made his fateful decision to the move the entire 3rd Corps forward about a half a mile to a peach orchard on the Sherfy farm at the Emmitsburg Road. He extended his line through a wheat field and on to Devil's Den. To protect the left flank, General Ward, commander of the 2nd Brigade, ordered Major Stoughton to move the 2nd U.S. Sharpshooters to the south along a dirt lane near the Slyder Farm.

This maneuver took about an hour and a half, as the terrain between the two positions included some dense woods and a swampy creek known as Plum Run. Major Stoughton took his time on this deployment for a couple of reasons. First, he wanted to make sure that there were no enemy soldiers hiding in these woods. Second, this slow

pace allowed the men to become familiar with the terrain and scout out good firing positions in the likely event that the regiment would have to retreat later on through the
same area.

Stoughton went to Captain McClure of Company D first to place his Maine men
to serve as the anchor at the right flank on the skirmish line behind a short wall. With
twenty-seven men it was the largest company in the regiment. The Slyder farm lane,
running almost east to west, faced to the south about 300 to 400 yards to the crest
of Warfield Ridge.[42] Stoughton then picked a small team
of about fifteen men from Companies E and H to scout
ahead to the top of that ridge. However, ten of these men
soon came streaming back as the 7,000 men of Confederate
Major General John B. Hood's division in three lines appeared at the same time, capturing five of the skirmishers.

Captain Jacob McClure

Completing a long and hot five-mile flanking maneuver, Hood's men were surprised to find any Union troops in
the vicinity as they had been led to believe by scouts that
the area was unoccupied. This news delayed the attack of
Hood's division for about half an hour, as Generals Hood
and Longstreet pondered their options. Their orders from
General Lee had been to attack north along the Emmitsburg Road, but now General
Hood wanted to continue to move to the left around Big Round Top. This suggestion
was denied. Near 4:00 p.m., the Confederate line began moving down the crest of Warfield Ridge towards the deadly fire of the sharpshooters.

Facing directly across from the Maine men in Company D and the Minnesota men
in Company A stood General Robertson's brigade of three Texas regiments (1st, 4th,
and 5th) and the 3rd Arkansas Regiment. The Texas brigade was one of the toughest in
the Confederate army, famous for its gallant charge in the "Cornfield" at Antietam. Men
from the 1st Texas were sent forward of the line as skirmishers. As they came within 200
yards of the sharpshooter's line, Companies D and A commenced an accurate fire that
forced the Texans to retreat. Ordered by Major Stoughton to move ahead to capture a
wounded soldier, Private Edwin Aldritt of Company A gave his canteen to his enemy.
"What regiment is that behind the wall?" asked the Texan. "We are the Second United
States Sharpshooters," replied Aldritt. "My God," remarked the Texan, "I never saw such
shooting."[43]

Following this brief pause, General Robertson then ordered his brigade to fix bayonets and charge the Sharpshooter line. While causing considerable casualties and forcing
the Confederates to break their formation, eventually the Texans outflanked Company D on the right, compelling the entire company to fall back. During this retreat,

according to Sergeant James Matthews, Captain McClure, Sergeant John Wade, Private John Allen, and Private James Bradley were wounded. Private Charles Wentworth of Rockland "skedaddled" and did not return to the regiment until the battle was over.[44]

The retreat of Company D also forced the Minnesotans of Company A to run for the rear. The four middle companies of the line (E,G,C, and H) also retreated, but in a more orderly fashion. As Robertson's orders were to maintain contact with the Emmitsburg Road on his left, this had the effect of splitting the Texas brigade. The 4th and 5th Texas continued to the right while the 3rd Arkansas and 1st Texas moved left. This created a domino effect of forcing two regiments in General Law's brigade, the 44th and 48th Alabama to slide into the gap created by the Texas brigade. It also pushed his other three units, the 4th, 47th, and 15th Alabama Regiments to the right of the 4th and 5th Texas.

This had profound consequences for the rest of the day's battle. Confederate General Benning's 1,400 man brigade of Georgians, entering the field behind Law's brigade, ended up following the 44th and 48th Alabama into Devils' Den instead of attacking the Federal flank at Little Round Top. This movement could have easily been corrected by General Hood but at the moment he was severely wounded in his left arm by an artillery fragment. Command of Hood's division fell to General Law, but he had moved so far to the right, that he did not learn of his promotion for some time.

Under good cover, the left two companies of the 2nd U.S. Sharpshooters (companies B and F), continued their deadly work as they retreated back and up the western slope of Big Round Top. In his report after the battle, Major Stoughton wrote,

> While they were advancing, the Second regiment did splendid execution, killing and wounding a great many. One regiment broke three times and rallied, before it would advance. I held my position until their line of battle was within one hundred yards of me and their skirmishers were pushing my right flank, when I ordered my men to fall back, firing as they retired. My left wing retreated up the hill and allowed the enemy to pass up the ravine, when they poured a destructive fire into his flank and rear.[45]

Forced by this fire to pay attention to his flank, Colonel William C. Oates pivoted his regiment, the 15th Alabama, to the right, climbing to the peak of Big Round Top. There, his men exhausted and out of water, he detailed two from each of his companies to gather all the canteens to find water. These men never returned as they were captured by twelve members of Company B.[46]

In all, the 2nd U.S. Sharpshooters suffered twenty-eight casualties (eleven of them from Company D) in this engagement.[47] Many of the Maine men of Company

D retreated back to Devil's Den and fought with members of the 2nd Brigade of the 3rd Corps, especially with friends in the 4th Maine Regiment. When General Benning's Georgia brigade did finally force the 4th Maine Regiment out of Devil's Den, some members of the Sharpshooters were captured. Several of the other members of the Sharpshooters ended up with Company B of the 20th Maine on that regiment's left flank. There they participated in the 20th Maine's famous bayonet charge down the slope of Little Round Top.

On July 3, except for a brief engagement in front of the Union 1st Corps line to silence a Confederate battery, the 2nd U.S. Sharpshooters were not engaged during Pickett's Charge. The end result of the 2nd Sharpshooter's labors during the second day at Gettysburg accomplished the regiment's finest two hours during the war. In a letter to Homer Stoughton, William Oates of the 15th Alabama wrote in 1888 on the 25th anniversary of the battle,

> The great service which you and your command did was, first, in changing my direction, and in drawing my regiment and the 47th Alabama away from the point of attack. You drew off and delayed this force of 1,000 men from falling on the Union left at the same time of attack of Law's other three regiments . . . and but for the service on your part I am confident that we would have swept away the Union line and captured Little Round Top, which would have won the battle for us . . . You and your command deserve a monument for turning the tide in favor of the Union cause.[48]

"INTO THE SLAUGHTER PEN"
4th Maine Regiment — *July 2, 1863, 4:15 — 5:30 p.m.*

Responding to President Lincoln's call for 75,000 volunteers following the beginning of hostilities at Fort Sumter in April of 1861, ten companies of infantrymen were organized from towns in Knox, Lincoln, and Waldo counties in Maine (four from Rockland, two from Belfast, and one each from Brooks, Searsport, Wiscasset, and Damariscotta) to form the 4th Maine Regiment. Hiram G. Berry, a former mayor of Rockland, was elected colonel. Originally enlisting for three months, while in camp at Fort Knox, the men were asked to reenlist for a three-year term. Most did, except for at number of men from Winterport in Company F.

The regiment, after two months of training, left the Pine Tree State on June 17, 1861 for Washington, D.C.. Along the way they stopped in New York City and marched down Broadway to city hall to receive the national flag and state flag from the Daughters of Maine in Brooklyn. Thanking the crowd assembled for their kindness, Colonel Berry, taking the flag, descended the platform to address his regiment: "'Shall this flag ever trail in the dust?' Loud cries of ' No, no! ' 'Will you defend it so long as you have a right arm? ' ' We will, we will ! ' shouted the men of the regiment, and a simultaneous shout of applause broke from the assembled thousands."[49]

Once in Virginia the regiment participated in most the battles of the Army of the Potomac for the next two years. At the First Battle of Bull Run in July of 1861, the regiment suffered 23 men killed, 27 men wounded, and 41 men missing. During the Peninsula Campaign and the Second Battle of Bull Run, the 4th Maine suffered further casualties while being heavily engaged. At the battles of Fredericksburg and Chancellorsville an additional 25 men were killed, 64 were wounded, and 43 reported missing. By the time they reached Gettysburg on the evening of July 1, 1863, the regiment was down to 314 men and 18 officers with Colonel Elijah Walker of Rockland in command.[50]

At about 9:00 p.m., Colonel Walker received an order from General Sickles to establish a picket line across the Emmitsburg Road, making some contact with Confederate pickets. However, the evening was quiet when the 4th Maine was relieved of picket duties by the 1st Massachusetts. Following the

Colonel Elijah Walker

reconnaissance by the 3rd Maine regiment around noon on the July 2, the 4th Maine took position to the extreme left of the new 3rd Corps line established when General Sickles ordered his controversial advance in the afternoon.

It was a strong position on a small hill (Houck's Ridge) just to the right of Devil's Den, a ravine dotted with huge boulders just to the west of a small creek called Plum Run.[51] On the other side of the creek, about 400 yards east, was the crest of Little Round Top. The 2nd U. S. Sharpshooters were posted another 300-400 yards south as a skirmish line. The 4th Maine was posted behind and to the left, in support of Captain James Smith's 4th New York Battery. To its right the other regiments of Ward's Second Brigade of the First Division of 3rd Corps were the 124th New York, the 86th New York, the 20th Indiana, and the 99th Pennsylvania. The men of the 4th Maine had not eaten a meal since the previous day, so a heifer was "drafted" from a field nearby and fires were lit on the hot afternoon. They did not have much time to eat the rare meat and drink their coffee.

At around 4:00 p.m., Smith's battery opened fire on Confederate positions to the south of Warfield Ridge.[52] Soon, Law's and Robertson's Confederate brigades were observed moving down from the ridge and forcing the Sharpshooters back. Colonel

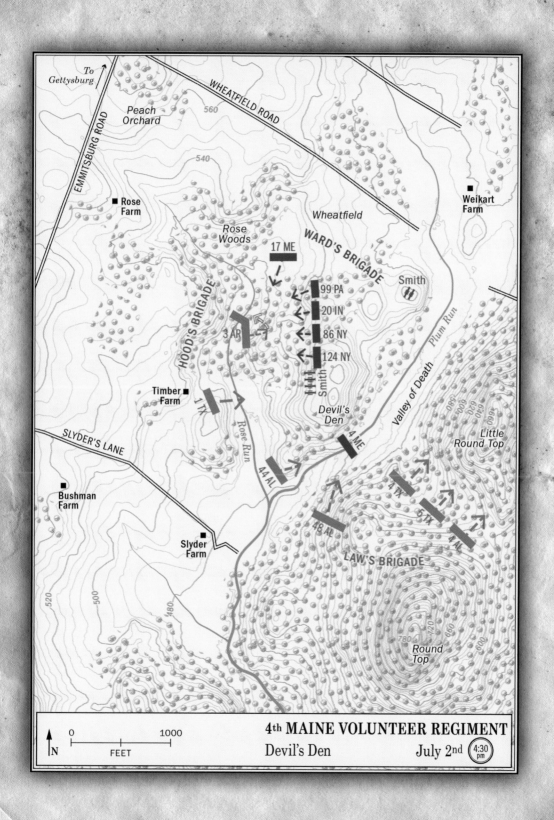

To
Gettysburg

WHEATFIELD ROAD

EMMITSBURG ROAD

Peach
Orchard

560

540

Rose
Farm

Rose
Woods

Wheatfield

WARD'S BRIGADE

Weikart
Farm

17 ME

99 PA

20 IN

Smith

HOOD'S BRIGADE

3 AR

86 NY

124 NY

Smith

Plum Run

Timber
Farm

1 TX

Devil's
Den

580
600
620
640
660

Little
Round Top

SLYDER'S LANE

Rose Run

4 ME

Valley of Death

44 AL

4 TX

48 AL

5 TX

4 AL

Bushman
Farm

LAW'S BRIGADE

Slyder
Farm

520

500

480

720
780
660
600

Round
Top

0   1000

FEET

N

4th MAINE VOLUNTEER REGIMENT

Devil's Den

July 2nd

4:30
pm

Walker received an order from General Ward through his adjutant to move from his position on Houck's Ridge to his left, past the large boulders of Devil's Den to the low ground of Plum Run Creek. Walker objected to this move because it would create a hole in the line of about 200 yards and leave the left flank of Smith's Battery unprotected, but he reluctantly obeyed after "remonstrating with all the power of speech I could command."[53]

Walker then sent a few skirmishers, commanded by Lieutenant Arthur Libby of Rockland, into the woods at his front and up toward the Round Tops to protect his left flank, but soon saw Colonel Strong Vincent's Brigade of the 5th Corps move up Little Round Top. Assuming that Vincent would post his own skirmishers down the slope, Walker recalled his advance in that direction. Thus he was not alerted when the 44th Alabama suddenly appeared at the edge of a wood of small pines on the left flank. Only his thinly manned Maine regiment stood in the way of a rebel flanking movement and possible defeat for the Army of the Potomac.

Luckily, the Alabama soldiers were disorganized after marching through the woods and undergrowth and its colonel, William F. Perry, stopped his men to align them into battle formation. The 4th Maine poured a withering fire into the 44th Alabama, forcing that unit to retire back into the woods with one fourth of its number either killed or wounded. Within minutes, Colonel Walker had to refuse his left flank to meet the fire of another oncoming Confederate regiment, the 48th Alabama. Barely sixty feet apart, the foes exchanged fire in an area now known as the "Slaughter Pen." The 48th Alabama made two more attacks but they were unable to move the 4th Maine. Colonel Walker was severely wounded when a Confederate bullet tore his Achilles tendon and then passed through his leg and killed his horse

Meanwhile, Smith's Battery had been overrun by the 1st Texas Regiment and this new development was threatening the right and rear of the 4th Maine. Colonel Walker, realizing that this position was key, ordered his men to retire about 100 yards, had them fix bayonets, and charged to the right, driving the Texans from Smith's guns in close hand-to-hand combat with the aid of the 99th Pennsylvania and the 124th New York. Many of the casualties suffered by the 4th Maine during the Battle of Gettysburg occurred here. Colonel Walker, hobbling on his one good leg, at one point was surrounded by rebel soldiers and had his sword wrenched from his hand, but his men saved him and the sword was recovered.

However, the 44th Alabama had returned to the field, assisted again by the 48th Alabama, and now, including the 17th and 2nd Georgia Regiments. It soon became apparent that the brigade would have to fall back to avoid annihilation or capture. Finally, General Ward gave the order to retire. Colonel Walker was unable to walk, but he was saved from capture by Sergeant Edger L. Mowry of Rockland and Corporal Freeman M. Robert of Jackson, who wrestled him from the hands of the enemy and carried him to the rear. His sword was taken for a second time and never recovered. Captain Edwin Libby took command of the regiment, as Major Ebenezer Whitcomb of Searsport, had been mortally wounded during the fight. Walker reported, "Our flag was pierced by thirty-two bullets and two pieces of shell, and its staff was shot off, but Sergt. Henry O. Ripley [of Rockland], its bearer, did not allow the color to touch the ground [keeping the promise made in New York City], nor did he receive a scratch, though all the others of the color guard were killed or wounded."[54]

On July 3, the regiment went into reserve behind the lines on Cemetery Ridge and did not participate in the repulse of Pickett's Charge. In all, the regiment suffered a 43% casualty rate (23 killed, 44 wounded, and 73 men missing or taken prisoner) during the Battle of Gettysburg. They had done enough.

"BAYONET"
20th Maine Regiment — *July 2, 1863, 4:30 — 5:30 p.m.*

No bands played, no parades were given, and no chest-thumping speeches were made when the 20th Maine Regiment went off to war. It was an orphan regiment, an afterthought, a rag-tag bunch of leftovers taken from every part of the state of Maine. When Maine answered President Lincoln's call for 300,000 volunteers in 1862, the 20th became the last three-year regiment of that year from Maine, 979 men (not quite a full regiment of 1,000) who had enlisted to become parts of the 16th, 17th, 18th, and 19th Maine Regiments but found themselves not needed to fill the rolls.

The men in the ten companies of the regiment were found to be from ten different counties of the state. Companies A, C, D, and F came from the farms of central and western Maine, from towns like Sidney, Solon, Waterville, and Freedom. Companies E, G, I, and K came from Maine's rugged coast, from Freeport to Winterport, Damariscotta to Waldoboro. Company B's men came from Piscataquis County — Foxcroft, Brownville, and Guilford mostly, while Company H was made up of lumberman and farmers from the northern part of the state, Aroostook County, from towns like Presque Isle, Houlton, Masardis, and Oxbow Plantation.

Except for the newly appointed colonel of the regiment, twenty-six year old Adelbert Ames of Rockland (an 1861 graduate of West Point) and Major Charles D. Gilmore of Bangor (who had commanded a company in the 7th Maine), no one in the regiment had any military experience. The regiment's second in command, Lieutenant Colonel Joshua L. Chamberlain of Brunswick, was a language and rhetoric professor at Bowdoin College, so not much was expected from him. This group desperately needed some training after mustering in at the end of August. However, there was barely time to teach the men how to march in a straight line before the regiment left the state, not even receiving weapons until reaching Washington, D.C., on September 7, 1862.

The situation then and there was grave. The Confederate army under General Robert E. Lee had just inflicted another embarrassing defeat on the Army of the Potomac at the Second Battle of Bull Run. Lee then decided to invade the North with his victorious Army of Northern Virginia. Bodies were needed to defend the capital, even if they were as unorganized and untrained as the 20th Maine. Marching as part of the 5th Corps, the 20th Maine moved toward Sharpsburg, Maryland, but did not participate in the Battle of Antietam, coming under fire for the first time three days later at Shepherdstown Ford (where Chamberlain had a horse shot out from under him, the first of many).

The march was especially hard on the untrained men of the 20th Maine and Colonel Ames was especially embarrassed by the regiment's performance. Once in camp, he became a hard taskmaster. The men of the regiment soon grew to hate him. Thomas

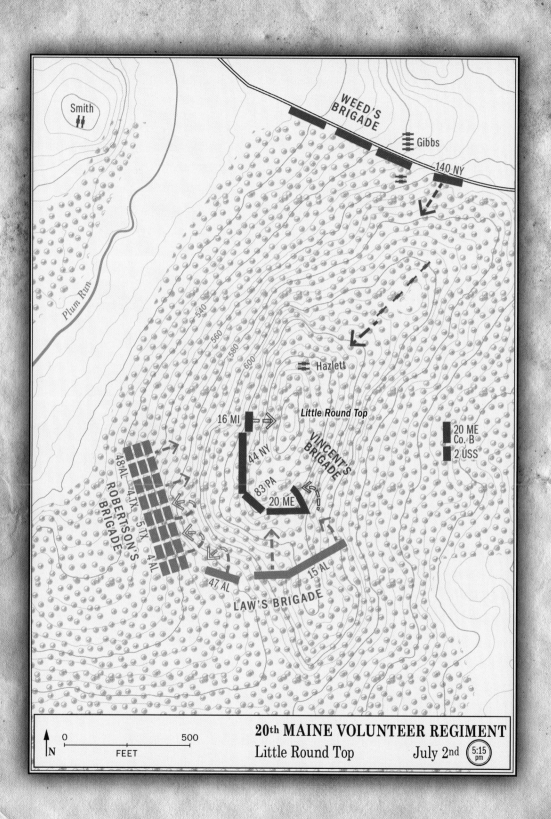

Smith

WEED'S BRIGADE

Gibbs

140 NY

Plum Run

540

560

580

600

Hazlett

Little Round Top

16 MI

44 NY

83 PA

20 ME

VINCENT'S BRIGADE

48 AL

4 TX

5 TX

4 AL

ROBERTSON'S BRIGADE

47 AL

15 AL

LAW'S BRIGADE

20 ME
Co. B

2 USS

N

0   500

FEET

20th MAINE VOLUNTEER REGIMENT

Little Round Top

July 2nd   5:15 pm

Chamberlain, the younger brother of Joshua, in October of 1862, wrote to his sister to describe the regiment's loathing, "I swear they will shoot him the first battle we are in," later writing, "Col. A will take the men out to drill & he will d'm them up hill and down." A few days later in another letter, Thomas complained, "I tell you he is about as savage a man as you ever saw."[55]

Eventually the men in the regiment began to take shape and grudgingly came to admire their colonel.[56] Moving into Virginia, the regiment went into battle at Fredericksburg, securing a position near the enemy's line. They were unable to do much but lay down under intense artillery and gunfire during another disastrous defeat at the hands of General Lee's men. Back across the Rappahannock River, they ran into some more unfortunate luck when a bad batch of small pox vaccine caused the regiment to be held

under quarantine. Hoping that the quarantine would be lifted in time to take part in the Chancellorsville campaign, Lt. Colonel Chamberlain suggested that if the regiment could do no more it might "give the enemy the small pox."[57] The only duty given, however, was to guard telegraph lines. Colonel Ames, exasperated by a lack of action, got himself promoted and the command of the 20th Maine fell to Chamberlain, who was himself promoted to colonel.

On the road to Pennsylvania as the Gettysburg campaign unfolded, the 20th Maine did take part in a small fight at Middleburg, Virginia. What followed was a great deal of marching, some days twenty miles or more, fi-

Lieutenant Colonel Joshua Chamberlain

nally reaching the outskirts of Gettysburg around midnight on July 1, 1863. On the morning of July 2, the regiment was moved from positions near Cemetery and Culp's Hills south to a line in support of 3rd Corps, which soon began marching forward toward the Emmittsburg Road.

As General Sickles left the rest of the army behind, General Gouverneur Warren, Chief of Engineers on General Meade's staff became worried about the two larger hills to the south of the Union line. He asked for and got permission from General Meade to go take a look. When he got to the top of the smaller hill, Little Round Top, he found something astonishing. There was no one there except for a small group of signal men. Realizing that this position perhaps was of prime importance (almost at the same time that Colonel William Oates of the 15th Alabama realized the same thing), General Warren frantically sent for help.

Intercepting a staff member, Colonel Strong Vincent, leader of the 3rd Brigade, 1st Division of the 5th Corps, learned of the crisis on Little Round Top. Under his own initiative, he led his brigade up the slope under fire from Confederate artillery and positioned his men, members of the 44th New York, 16th Michigan, 83rd Pennsylvania, and the 20th Maine. As he climbed the hill, Colonel Chamberlain was with his brothers Thomas and John (who was there working with the Christian Commission to help with the wounded). A shell exploded nearby. "Boys, I don't like this," exclaimed Colonel Chamberlain, "Another such shot might make it hard for mother," as he ordered Thomas to go to the rear of the regiment, and John to look for a good place to collect the wounded.[58]

The 20th Maine was posted down the southern slope of Little Round Top to the left of the brigade's line. Soon Colonel Vincent appeared and told Chamberlain, "This is the left of the Union line. You understand. You are to hold this ground at all costs!"[59] Then Vincent left (to shortly be mortally wounded near the crest of the hill). Chamberlain then ordered the forty-four men of Company B, led by Captain Walter G. Morrill of Williamsburg (now Northeast Piscataquis), to the left to cover the regiments open flank. Captain Morrill found a small wall in the woods about 150 yards to the east where he posted his company. Formed in line, the rest of the 20th Maine, with about 300 men waited, it was about 4:45 p.m. They did not have long to wait.

Captain Walter G. Morrill

The first Confederate attack hit on the right of the 20th Maine, as the 4th Alabama, 4th Texas, and 5th Texas Regiments began climbing the hill. Most of this first charge fell upon the 83rd Pennsylvania and 44th New York Regiments and it was beaten back. As the Confederates regrouped for a second charge, they were joined on their right by seven companies of the 47th Alabama and Colonel Oates's 15th Alabama, who had been on the crest of Big Round Top.[60] These two regiments attacked the right flank and center of the 20th Maine's line, but the Maine men got off the first volley. Falling back, the 15th Alabama prepared for another charge and began moving to the right to find some open space. Sensing this movement, Colonel Chamberlain had his men refuse their line to the left to meet this new threat. No longer in a double line, the Maine regiment was stretched as thin as it could get.

For the next hour or so, the two regiments engaged in a desperate fight along the slopes of this small hill in Pennsylvania. Colonel Oates counted five separate charges. On the last charge, his men were able to push the left flank of the 20th Maine, commanded by Major Ellis Spear, back to the right almost forcing these men upon the rear of the

Major Edward B. Knox — Ellsworth Avenger

As the 20th Maine was locked in a death grip with the 15th Alabama on the southern slope of Little Round Top, the 44th New York regiment, also of the 3rd Brigade, 1st Division of 5th Corps, was at the top of the hill fighting elements of Robertson's Texas and Alabama brigades. One of the officers of the Regiment, Major Edward B. Knox, was a native of Maine. Born in Eastport in 1838, Knox moved to Illinois in the late 1850s. There he joined a small drill unit known as the National Guard Cadets.

Soon Elmer Ellsworth, a former law clerk for Abraham Lincoln, joined the group as its leader, renaming it the Zouave Cadets and dressing the unit in flamboyant French Algerian-inspired military uniforms. He made the Zouave Cadets the most famous drill team in the country. Ellsworth and Knox became close friends. When the war started they formed the 11th New York Regiment, soon known as "Ellsworth's Zouaves," recruited from New York City volunteer fire companies. Ellsworth was shot by a hotel proprietor in Alexandria, Virginia, on May 24, 1861, becoming the first officer to be killed in the war. Many of the men, including Knox, returned, after their enlistment period of ninety days was up, to New York to form the 44th New York Regiment, known as "The People's Ellsworth Regiment" or the "Ellsworth Avengers."

Knox served in the 44th New York until October of 1864; he was wounded twice during battles in Virginia. In 1890, while going door to door to raise funds for the Illinois National Guard in Chicago, he died of a stroke. Thousands of mourners attended his funeral.

20th Maine's right flank, the line now resembled a hairpin. Here Colonel Oates reached a large boulder where he thought for a moment that he had actually turned the Union army flank. However, the Maine men hit back, forcing Oates and his men to retreat. His men had never before been defeated, but he did not have enough men to prevail.

At this point, Chamberlain's men were running dangerously low on ammunition. Sensing that another attack would engulf his regiment and remembering Vincent's order to hold at all costs, Chamberlain came to a momentous decision. Lieutenant Holman Melcher of Topsham came up to the colonel to ask permission to go ahead of the line and gather some of the wounded who were crying for aid. Chamberlain hesitated then informed Melcher that he was about to order a bayonet charge. Anticipating the colonel's order, the remaining 200 men of the 20th Maine were almost over the line before Chamberlain shouted, "Bayonet!" Melcher, knowing the colonel's intent, was out in front.

On the left, Major Spear had not heard the order but seeing the center and right of the regiment move down the slope, he also ordered a charge of the left wing. All of this happened to coincide with Colonel Oates's decision to withdraw his exhausted troops, but before he could pass the word to his men, the 20th Maine came charging down the hill. On the far left, still behind the little stone wall, Captain Morrill and Company B had been joined by several members of the 2nd U.S. Sharpshooters. As the Alabama regiment began to retreat they found themselves attacked from the left by men with different colored uniforms. Thinking that the Union line had been reinforced, the retreat of the 15th Alabama became a rout. As Chamberlain ran down the hill with his men he approached a Confederate officer who fired his pistol at him. Either missing or misfiring, the man then handed over his sword and pistol to the colonel in surrender.[61]

While Colonel Chamberlain reported the capture of 400 Confederates, the number was probably closer to 200. His regiment had suffered 130 men killed or wounded. Meanwhile, the crest of Little Round Top had been reinforced with artillery and infantry and was secured from further attack. At about 9:00 p.m., the 20th Maine was ordered to the top of Big Round Top, where it held that position until relieved the following day. About twenty-five additional prisoners were taken, including one of Confederate General Law's staff officers. The regiment, now covered in glory and much the talk of the rest of the army, moved to a position behind the left center of the Union line on Cemetery Ridge, where they did not take part in the repulse of Pickett's Charge. They, like the 4th Maine in Devil's Den, had done enough. Not bad for a bunch of leftovers.[62]

"THE LAST CARTRIDGE WAS GONE"
17th Maine Regiment — *July 2, 1863, 4:45 — 6:40 p.m.*

The 17th Maine Regiment mustered into service on August 18, 1862, having filled its ranks three weeks earlier, under the command of Colonel Thomas A. Roberts, a 45-year-old house painter and wallpaper hanger from Portland, Maine (Roberts had some military experience as a captain of a local militia company). His son, Charles W. Roberts served as adjutant of the regiment. Second in command was Lieutenant Colonel Charles B. Merrill, a lawyer from Portland, with George W. West of Massachusetts as major (although born in Massachusetts, West had settled in Aroostook County, where he had been in the lumber business). West had served previously as a captain in the 10th

Maine Regiment. Most of the regiment was made up of men from Androscoggin (152 men), Cumberland (398 men), Franklin (84 men), Oxford (168 men), and York (178 men) counties with a scattering from eight others.[63]

Marching through the streets of Portland to the cheers of an enthusiastic crowd, the 17th Maine left Maine on August 21, 1862 arriving in Washington, D.C., two days later having survived the unpleasant experience of being loaded into box cars as they passed through Baltimore. There they went on to training, missing both the Second Battle of Bull Run and the Battle of Antietam. Like most of the Maine regiments that were recruited in 1862, the 17th Maine went into camp without tents or proper shelter. This caused much sickness in the regiment, leading to the loss of more than one hundred men due to death or disability.

The regiment was lightly engaged at the Battle of Fredericksburg in December of 1862, suffering three killed and seventeen wounded. At the Battle of Chancellorsville in May of 1863, Lieutenant Colonel Merrill led the regiment, as Colonel Roberts was absent on sick leave. This was the first real test of combat for the regiment. Positioned at a place south of the Chancellor House in support of a battery, the 17th Maine repulsed a Confederate charge and took many prisoners. Eventually, as the brigade was forced to

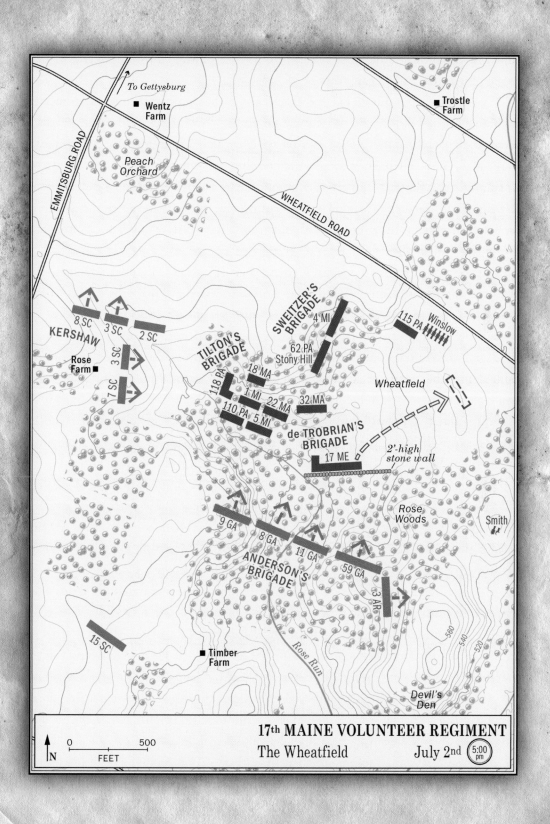

To Gettysburg

■ Wentz Farm

■ Trostle Farm

EMMITSBURG ROAD

Peach Orchard

WHEATFIELD ROAD

SWEITZER'S BRIGADE

4 MI

115 PA   Winslow

8 SC   3 SC   2 SC

KERSHAW

Rose Farm ■   3 SC

7 SC

TILTON'S BRIGADE

62 PA Stony Hill

118 PA   18 MA

1 MI   22 MA   32 MA

Wheatfield

110 PA   5 MI

de TROBRIAN'S BRIGADE

17 ME

2'-high stone wall

Rose Woods

Smith

9 GA

8 GA   11 GA

59 GA

3 AR

ANDERSON'S BRIGADE

15 SC

■ Timber Farm

Rose Run

Devil's Den

0   500

FEET

N

17th MAINE VOLUNTEER REGIMENT

The Wheatfield   July 2nd   5:00 pm

retreat from this position, the 17th Maine was the last regiment to withdraw. During the battle, the regiment suffered heavy losses, including 11 dead, 59 wounded, and 41 taken prisoner, for a total of 111 casualties.

Breaking camp on June 11, 1863, from Falmouth, Virginia, the regiment began its march northward. On June 25, the regiment marched thirty miles, its one-day record for the entire war, reaching the Monocacy River in Maryland. From there, the march continued through Point of Rocks, Jefferson Village, Middletown, Frederick City, Taneytown, and Emmitsburg. As part of Colonel Philippe Régis Denis de Keredern de Trobriand's 3rd Brigade of General Birney's 1st Division of the 3rd Corps, the regiment received orders early on the morning of July 2 to march rapidly to Gettysburg from Emmitsburg, arriving there in the late forenoon.[64] Making a quick meal of hardtack and coffee, the regiment soon pushed forward when General Sickles made his decision to advance the 3rd Corps. Lieutenant Colonel Merrill was still in command of the regiment, as Colonel Roberts had applied for permanent leave due to illness in early June of 1863.[65]

Initially placed to the south of Sherfy's peach orchard, near the Rose family barn, the 17th Maine was moved double-quick to a good position at the south end of a large wheat field behind a short stone wall at the edge of Rose Woods. This movement was ordered when Colonel de Trobriand discovered that there was a huge gap between his brigade and the 2nd Brigade of General Ward positioned at Devil's Den. Connected to the rest of the brigade on its right flank, the 17th Maine's new left flank was "in the air." The regiment could not quite stretch far enough to connect with the right flank of Ward's brigade.

As Confederate General Benning's brigade attempted to break through Ward's men in Devil's Den, the left flank of the 3rd Arkansas Regiment found itself being enfiladed by fire from the 17th Maine. Turning north to meet this threat, the men from Arkansas made an effort to break the line of the men behind the stone wall, but the Razorbacks were thrown back with heavy losses. Now a new threat developed. Confederate General George "Tige" Anderson's Georgia brigade of Hood's division entered the fight. These men were veterans and were not used to being stopped.

As the 11th and 8th Georgia hit the 17th Maine's line, Lt. Colonel Merrill noticed that a small gap had developed between his line on the right and the 115th Pennsylvania and the 8th New Jersey. He swung his right three companies, H, K, and C, around to create a salient angle so that when the 8th Georgia moved to this gap, they were hit by enfilading fire. At the stone wall, a desperate struggle ensued with hand-to-hand combat and bayonets. "Tige" Anderson finally withdrew his brigade back to wait for reinforcements.

At about 5:30 p.m., those reinforcements arrived. Confederate General Joseph Kershaw's South Carolina brigade of Major General Lafayette McLaws' division attacked from the west. General Anderson then renewed his attack from the south, throwing his men at the stone wall. Soon the South Carolinians had pushed the rest of de Trobriand's brigade

Brigadier General John C. Caldwell — No Troops Had Done Better

John Caldwell was born in Vermont in 1833. Highly educated (as a graduate of Amherst College), he moved to Maine in 1855 and became the principal of the Washington Academy in East Machias. With no military experience, at the age of 28, he was elected colonel of the 11th Maine Regiment. During the Peninsula Campaign he was appointed brigadier general, taking command of the 1st Brigade of the 1st Division of the 2nd Corps. He received wounds at Antietam and Fredericksburg, taking command of the 1st Division following the Battle of Chancellorsville.

No division commander at the Battle of Gettysburg performed better and got a rawer deal than Caldwell. Ordered into the Wheatfield on July 2nd to shore up the collapsing 3rd Corps line, Caldwell quickly (within ten minutes) got his division moving and into line, including an impressive facing-by-the-rear deployment, to conduct the largest assault by the Union army of the three-day battle, sweeping the field of Confederate soldiers. However, lacking support on his right flank, Caldwell's division was forced to retreat in some disorder. General George Sykes, commander of the 5th Corps, criticized Caldwell's handling of his troops following the battle. Colonel Charles H. Morgan, Chief of Staff of 2nd Corps, later wrote, "Subsequent investigation showed that no troops on the field had done better."* Although exonerated from any blame, Caldwell's reputation was damaged. The following year he was relieved of his command.

After the war Caldwell served in the honor guard for President Lincoln's funeral train, was elected to the Maine Legislature, and became U.S. Council in several Latin American countries. He died in Calais, Maine, in 1912 and is buried in St. Stephen, New Brunswick.

The Gettysburg Campaign: A Study in Command, by Edwin Coddington (1963), page 751.

back, creating a dangerous situation for the Maine men. Now the Confederates held positions to the rear of the regiment. Left alone, the 17th Maine was ordered back, although the men were loath to leave their fine position behind that stone wall. The situation was desperate; another push by the Confederates would break the Union line.

At this point, General David Birney, commander of the 1st Division, came on the scene. Realizing the grave nature of the moment, he placed himself at the front of the 17th Maine and ordered a charge back across the trampled down wheat to the stone wall. Somehow it worked and the Confederate advance was temporarily stopped. Moving back to the middle of the field, Birney ordered the 17th Maine to hold that position and keep the enemy back. At this point he was notified that General Sickles had been wounded and that he was now in charge of the 3rd Corps. Birney left the Maine men where they stood in the open field with "no protection of any sort."[66]

Several times, Confederate troops broke into the Wheatfield only to be driven back. The men were now very short of ammunition, when "the last cartridge was gone . . . the men were told by the commanding officer that the Seventeenth would stay there and hold the ground with the bayonet until the last man had fallen."[67]

Finally, at about 6:40 p.m., General John Caldwell (of East Machias) and his division of the 2nd Corps arrived, marching rapidly from its position on Cemetery Ridge and taking the position under fire to relieve the 17th Maine. Colonel Merrill, in a letter to the Assistant Adjutant General of Maine on July 5, 1863, noted, "In the Color Guard of ten, but three escaped uninjured; our ammunition being exhausted, and fresh troops having arrived to take our places we were ordered to withdraw from the field, which we did in good order. A new line was formed but a short distance to the rear, where we bivouacked for the night."[68]

On July 3, the regiment was posted to extreme left of the line on Cemetery Ridge, suffering two killed and ten wounded. In all the regiment suffered about 130 casualties of the 350 men engaged in the battle. For over two hours the 17th Maine had withstood the frantic attacks of some of the best troops in General Longstreet's corps. They had held in the "Bloody Wheatfield."

"WRAPPED IN A VORTEX OF FIRE"
3rd Maine Regiment — *July 2, 1863, 5:45 — 7:00 p.m.*

Returning from their reconnaissance at Pitzer's Woods, Colonel Lakeman's men of the 3rd Maine rested and took a quick meal from anything they could find in their haversacks. They now numbered only 162 men and officers after their midday excursion. Soon they received orders to advance. However, the 3rd Maine did not follow the other men of Ward's brigade into Devil's Den but were instead attached to the 1st Brigade of the 3rd Corps under the command of Brigadier General Charles K. Graham and positioned at the Sherfy Peach Orchard along the Emmitsburg Road.

Being now the smallest regiment in this position, the 3rd Maine was sent forward to the south and west about 250 yards to serve as skirmishers. At around 4:00 p.m., Colonel Lakeman, scanning to the south with his glass saw the gleaming bayonets and lines of infantry belonging to Hood's division of Longstreet's corps as they began their attack on the Round Tops and Devil's Den. He sent word back to Captain George E. Randolph,

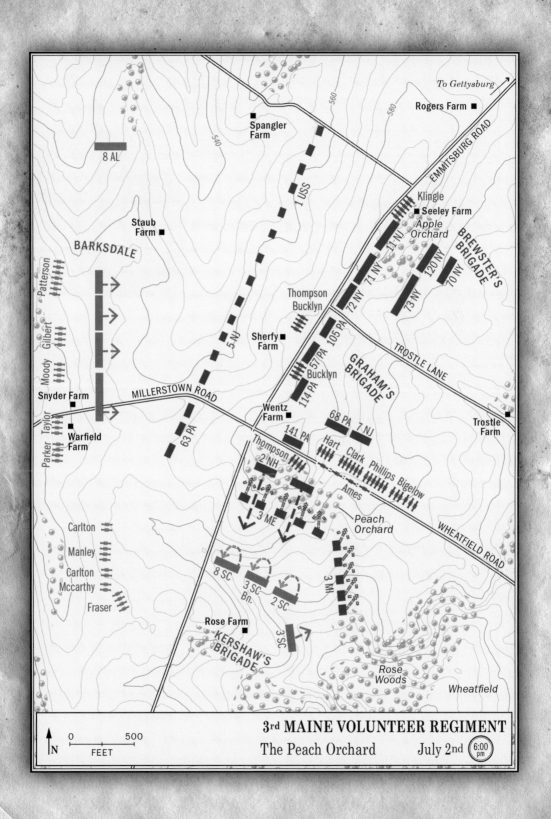

To Gettysburg

Rogers Farm

EMMITSBURG ROAD

Spangler Farm

560

560

8 AL

1 USS

Klingle
Seeley Farm
Apple Orchard

BREWSTER'S BRIGADE

Staub Farm

540

BARKSDALE

Patterson

11 NJ

72 NY

71 NY

73 NY

120 NY

70 NY

Gilbert

5 NJ

Thompson Bucklyn

Moody

Sherfy Farm

105 PA

TROSTLE LANE

57 PA

GRAHAM'S BRIGADE

Snyder Farm

MILLERSTOWN ROAD

Bucklyn

114 PA

Parker Taylor

Warfield Farm

63 PA

Wentz Farm

68 PA   7 NJ

Trostle Farm

141 PA

Hart   Clark   Phillips   Bigelow

Thompson
2 NH

Ames

Carlton

3 ME

Peach Orchard

Manley

WHEATFIELD ROAD

Carlton
Mccarthy

8 SC

3 SC Bn.

2 SC

3 MI

Fraser

Rose Farm

3 SC

KERSHAW'S BRIGADE

Rose Woods

Wheatfield

3rd MAINE VOLUNTEER REGIMENT
The Peach Orchard   July 2nd (6:00 pm)

N

0   500
FEET

Chief of the 3rd Corps Artillery, who then began to fire shot and shell toward the enemy. Captain Randolph's five batteries were joined by the four batteries of the 1st Volunteer Brigade of the Artillery Reserve. The combined firepower and thundering noise of these batteries must have been impressive to the men of the 3rd Maine as the shelling commenced directly over their heads.

Colonel Moses B. Lakeman

However, by 5:30 p.m., Confederate General Kershaw's brigade of McLaw's division moved forward to attack the Union line in the Wheatfield. The left flank of this brigade, the 2nd, 3rd, and 8th South Carolina Regiments, moved to the northeast, coming into contact with the 3rd Maine pushing them back to the Peach Orchard. Seeing this advance, Colonel Edward Bailey of the 2nd New Hampshire got permission from General Graham to charge the Confederate line. This temporarily stopped Kershaw's men and allowed the 3rd Maine skirmishers to retreat with few losses.

However, Confederate Colonel Edward P. Alexander's artillery battalion had moved to a position about 500 yards to the west and began pounding the Peach Orchard. Confederate General William Barksdale then released his Mississippi brigade toward the Emmitsburg Road, quickly breaking through Graham's line. This forced Colonel Lakeman to turn the 3rd Maine to the west to face this new development, just as Kershaw's men renewed their attack from the south, leaving the 3rd Maine to face fire from two directions.

The 141st Pennsylvania and the 3rd Michigan then joined the 3rd Maine and the 2nd New Hampshire in a valiant attempt to hold back Kershaw's South Carolinians to give the artillery time to retire. These men were now "wrapped in a vortex of fire."[69] Every man in the 3rd Maine's color guard was killed or wounded, including Captain John C. Keene of Leeds (who was pierced by four bullets) and 1st Lieutenant Henry Penniman of Winthrop (who was severely wounded in the leg), as were about one-third of the rest of men in the regiment. Unable to maintain this position further, the regiment retired to the east without its flag, leaving its dead and wounded on the field. In all on July 2, the 3rd Maine suffered 122 dead, wounded, or missing — a 58% casualty rate.

In a letter to Maine's Adjutant General, Colonel Lakemen praised his men,

> I am proud to state that the Regiment, though very small, sustained
> its reputation as one of the best fighting regiments in the army. They
> were chosen to open the engagement on the left of the line on the 2nd

inst. And the heroic daring displayed by them, when confronting ten times their number, is the source of universal admiration by the commanding General, and throughout the entire Corps, for myself, I cannot say too much in their praise.[70]

Indeed, General Sickles himself reportedly said, "the little Third Maine saved the Army today."[71] Sleeping on their arms that night, the next day the 3rd and 4th Maine took positions behind the main line on Cemetery Ridge, but did not take part in the repulse of Pickett's Charge.

"HOLD THE POSITION AT ALL HAZARDS"
Dow's 6th Maine Battery — *July 2, 1863, 6:00 — 8:00 p.m.*

Recruited from Aroostook, Waldo, and York counties, the 6th Maine Battery mustered into service on New Year's Day in 1862, under the command of Captain Freeman McGilvery of Stockton. George H. Smith of Hodgdon and Edwin B. Dow of Portland enlisted as 1st Lieutenants.[72] The battery did some training in Augusta and Portland before being moved to the defense of Washington, D.C., in April. There the men received additional training in heavy guns at several forts surrounding the city. Fearing a possible attack on the capital by "Stonewall" Jackson, as he began his famous valley campaign, the men of the 6th Battery were finally given their proper weapons — four 12-pound Napoleons and two 3-inch ordnance rifled guns, along with all the necessary horses, ammunition, and caissons.

On August 9, 1862, the battery took part in its first fight at the Battle of Cedar Mountain, under the overall command of Major General Nathaniel Banks. Posted near the extreme left of the Union line, the battery repulsed several charges of Jackson's men. However, after six hours of fighting, the army was forced to retire. At the Second Battle of Bull Run in late August, the 6th Maine Battery was almost captured, having barely fired a shot during the Federal rout and losing two of its six guns.

After Second Bull Run, the battery received some recruits and guns to replace those lost. At Antietam, the 6th Maine was posted to the rear to guard a bridge and was not involved in the fight and also did not participate in the Battle of Fredericksburg. By this time Captain McGilvery had been promoted to lieutenant colonel. Lieutenant Dow took command of the 6th Maine Battery. Following the reorganization of the federal artillery after the Battle of Chancellorsville, the battery became part of the 4th Volunteer Brigade of the Artillery Reserve, McGilvery taking command of the 1st Volunteer Brigade.

Now down to little more than 100 men, the battery was reduced to four 12-pound Napoleons. Commencing its movement to Gettysburg on June 13, 1863, the battery arrived there at about 8:00 a.m. on July 2 and parked on a field near the Taneytown Road, staying in position there for most of the morning and afternoon. The situation on the field had become desperate. Confederate General Barksdale's Mississippi Brigade had broken through the 3rd Corps line at the Peach Orchard. To his left, General Cadmus M. Wilcox and his men from Hill's 3rd Corps were marching in support. Although rebel troops had not been able to take Little Round Top, they had also broken through at Devil's Den and the Wheatfield, forcing General Caldwell's division back toward Cemetery Ridge. It looked for a few moments that the entire left flank of the Union army was about to collapse.

McGilvery, it seems, was everywhere on the field. He noticed a huge gap in the final Union line between the 2nd Corps on Cemetery Ridge and the 5th Corps on Little Round Top. The only artillery he had at the moment was the 9th Massachusetts Battery, posted near the Trostle house, commanded by Captain John Bigelow of Brighton. This battery was under fire for the first time. Riding up to the battery and needing to buy time to form another line to the rear, McGilvery shouted, "Captain Bigelow, there is not an infantryman back of you along the whole line from which Sickles moved out. You must remain where you are and hold your position at all hazards, and sacrifice your battery, if need be, until at least I can find some batteries to put in position and cover you. The enemy are coming down on you now."[73]

Colonel Freeman McGilvery —
Happy McGilvery Day!

Did you know that the 120th Maine State Legislature in 2001 designated the first Saturday of September of each year as "Freeman McGilvery Day?" Thus, the legislature finally honored one of Maine's greatest, and mostly forgotten, heroes of the Battle of Gettysburg. McGilvery was born in Prospect, Maine, in 1823. In Brazil as a ship master when the Civil War began, McGilvery returned to Maine to organize the 6th Maine Battery. Promoted to major in February of 1863, he was given command of the First Brigade of the Artillery Reserve. On the road to Gettysburg in June of 1863, he was promoted to lieutenant colonel.

On the afternoon of July 2, 1863, as the Federal line in the Wheatfield and Peach Orchard collapsed, McGilvery noticed a hole in the reserve line. Gathering as many artillery fieldpieces as he could, he filled the gap along Plum Run and held back the Confederate charge. On the third day of the battle, he ignored a direct order by General Winfield Hancock to fire his cannon during the Confederate bombardment. Instead he held his ammunition until Pickett's charge, causing massive casualties that contributed much to the repulse of the Confederate forces.

Promoted to full colonel and then placed in command as Chief of Artillery of the 10th Corps, McGilvery continued to perform with distinction. Slightly wounded in the hand at the Battle of Deep Bottom (August 1864), McGilvery died on September 3, 1864, of an overdose of chloroform during surgery to amputate a finger. He is buried in the Village Cemetery in Searsport, Maine.

Loading his cannon with double canister, Bigelow blew huge holes into the on-rushing ranks of the 21st Mississippi regiment, buying McGilvery almost thirty minutes while eventually losing four of his six cannon. McGilvery then collected cannon from several retreating batteries and called up the 6th Maine Battery from the rear which arrived on the scene at about 7:00 p.m. Setting up a line behind Plum Run Creek in full view of the enemy, McGilvery ordered Lieutenant Dow to "hold the position at all hazards."[74]

For the next hour, the Plum Run line held. Although several batteries to the right ran out of ammunition and were forced to retire. Both the 6th Maine Battery and the 5th Massachusetts Battery stood their ground, firing coolly with precision. The Maine battery fired an incredible 244 rounds of ammunition during this action, suffering eight wounded. By 8:00 p.m., Barksdale's charge had been turned back (Barksdale himself was wounded in the knee, got a cannonball to the foot and was finally felled by a chest wound, dying the next day in a Union field hospital). The gap had been plugged.

The following day, having replenished its supplies, the 6th Maine reported again to Colonel McGilvery for duty, this time in a line of 39 artillery pieces. While mostly hidden from view by Confederate artillery, McGilvery's line contributed heavily to the repulse of Pickett's Charge on July 3rd. The 6th Maine Battery fired 139 rounds during the day and suffered five casualties, all wounded.

"I'LL STAY HERE, GENERAL, UNTIL HELL FREEZES OVER"
19th Maine Regiment — *July 2, 1863, 7:30 — 9:00 p.m.*

Almost a third of the men in the 19th Maine Regiment were from Waldo County, with Kennebec, Somerset, Knox, and Sagadahoc counties also represented. Under the command of Colonel Frederick D. Sewell of Bath, who had served on the staff of General O. O. Howard and second in command, Francis E. Heath of Waterville, who had been a captain in the 3rd Maine Regiment, the 19th Maine was organized and mustered in at Bath, before making the trip to Washington, D.C., in late August of 1862. There the regiment was ordered to garrison some forts and receive training, including some training in artillery drill.

On September 30, 1862, the regiment was ordered to Harper's Ferry, Virginia, where it stayed in camp until the Fredericksburg campaign. In early December the regiment was assigned the duty of guarding the road from Belle Plain to Falmouth. One day the men marched in a cold rain that turned to snow then went into camp overnight with very little shelter, "this exposure killed more men of this regiment than any battle it ever engaged in."[75] The 19th Maine participated in the advance at the Battle of Fredericksburg on the army's right flank but saw little action and retreated back to camp in Falmouth on December 15, 1862.

In February of 1863, Colonel Sewell resigned his commission due to ill health and Lt. Colonel Heath was promoted to colonel and became the regimental commander. That same month, 1st Lieutenant Joseph Nichols of Phippsburg faced court martial charges. Nichols had attempted to resign from the service because he did not approve of President Lincoln's Emancipation Proclamation, which had gone into effect on January 1, 1863. As a Democrat back in Phippsburg, Nichols had enlisted for the purpose of saving the Union. He friends there had accused him of being an abolitionist, fighting to free the slaves. Nichols felt that by making this protest, he would set the record straight

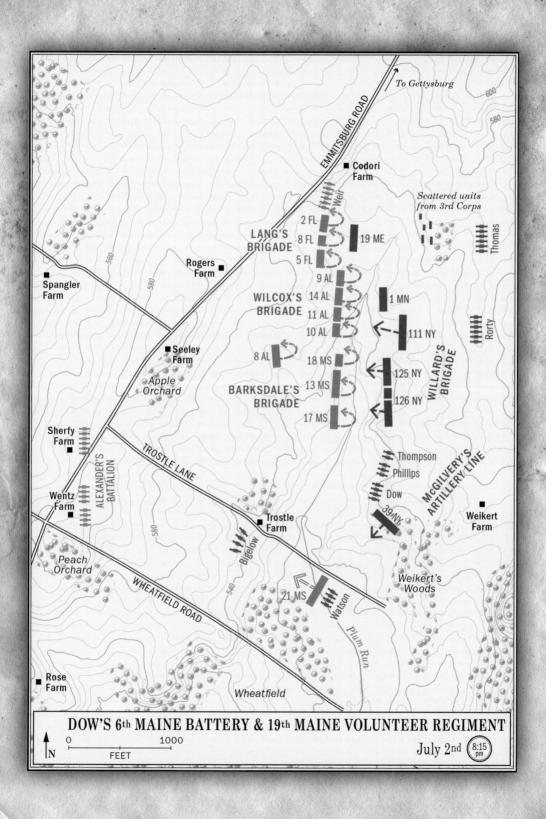

To Gettysburg

Codori Farm

Scattered units from 3rd Corps

Thomas

EMMITSBURG ROAD

Weir

2 FL

8 FL

5 FL

19 ME

LANG'S BRIGADE

Rogers Farm

9 AL

14 AL

1 MN

Spangler Farm

560

580

WILCOX'S BRIGADE

11 AL

10 AL

111 NY

Rorty

Seeley Farm

8 AL

18 MS

125 NY

WILLARD'S BRIGADE

Apple Orchard

BARKSDALE'S BRIGADE

13 MS

126 NY

17 MS

Sherfy Farm

TROSTLE LANE

Thompson

Phillips

McGILVERY'S ARTILLERY LINE

ALEXANDER'S BATTALION

Dow

Wentz Farm

580

Trostle Farm

39 NY

Weikert Farm

Peach Orchard

540

Bigelow

Weikert's Woods

WHEATFIELD ROAD

21 MS

Watson

Plum Run

Rose Farm

Wheatfield

DOW'S 6th MAINE BATTERY & 19th MAINE VOLUNTEER REGIMENT

0   1000

FEET

N

July 2nd (8:15 pm)

on his reasons for joining the army. He expected a reprimand, but did not expect that his resignation would be accepted and wished to stay in the service. Instead, his resignation letter came back from headquarters with orders to arrest him and place him in the guard house. Captain William H. Fogler of Belfast defended him before the court martial, but Nichols was cashiered. "He was a pleasant and lovable man and the officers and a great many of the men were very fond of him. He left the regiment regretted by all who knew him."[76]

The regiment did not participate in the Battle of Chancellorsville, getting the same telegraph guard duty as the 20th Maine Regiment. Beginning the first leg of the march north to Gettysburg, the regiment left its camp on the Rappahannock River on June 15, 1863. John Day Smith of Litchfield, the regimental historian and former private in the regiment, related in his book an amusing incident that occurred during a night march towards Thoroughfare Gap on June 20:

> The march took us across the old Bull Run battlefield where many ev-
> idences of the battles of former years were visible. Parts of human skeletons
> were seen protruding from the ground and splintered trees were upon every
> side. The last part of the march was very trying and in the darkness the boys
> of the Regiment stumbled over stones and into ditches. They knew from
> talk in the Regiment that we were bound for Thoroughfare Gap, but no
> one seemed to know how far away that place was. While the Regiment was
> plodding along, slowly picking its way in the dark, one of the boys fell into
> a deep ditch and when inquired of as to what he was doing down there he
> answered back, "Boys, here's the gap. I've stopped it up."[77]

The regiment arrived at Gettysburg at 3:00 a.m. on the morning of July 2, 1863, going into position on Cemetery Ridge just south of a small group of trees and almost opposite the Codori farm house east of the Emmitsburg Road. With the 1st Minnesota, 15th Massachusetts, and 82nd New York, the regiment was part of General William Harrow's 1st Brigade of General John Gibbon's 2nd Division of General Winfield Scott Hancock's 2nd Corps. The 19th Maine was the only Maine regiment in the 2nd Corps, bringing 405 men to the field.

As General Sickles made his impetuous move with the 3rd Corps in advance of the entire army, General Hancock was forced to move his line to try to fill gaps. When the 3rd Corps became heavily engaged after 4:00 p.m., Hancock sent his 1st Division, ably commanded by General John C. Caldwell of Maine, to the south to assist the 3rd Corps in its fight against the Confederate flanking movement. This forced General Hancock and General Meade to change the formation of remaining troops on Cemetery Ridge.

Hancock personally positioned the 19th Maine. Riding up, he found the last man on the left of the regiment, who happened to be Private George Durgan of Bowdoinham in Company F, moved him forward about fifty feet and said, "Will you stay here?" Durgin, who was a short and heavy man replied, "I'll stay here, General, until hell freezes over." Hancock smiled as he remounted his horse and ordered Colonel Heath to dress the regiment to the right of Private Durgin.[78]

However, the line of the 2nd Corps here was very thin. To the immediate left of the 19th Maine, the 1st Minnesota (which had quite a few native Maine sons) was about 250 yards away. To its right was the 5th U.S. Battery commanded by Lieutenant Gulian Wier.[79] As Confederate General Barksdale's Mississippi brigade began breaking through the 3rd Corps line, he was joined by the Alabama Brigade of General Wilcox and the Florida Brigade of General Lang, both from Hill's 3rd Corps, on his left. As these troops crossed the Emmitsburg Road with overwhelming force, the right flank of the Union 3rd Corps under the command of General Andrew Humphreys fell back in disorder.

Colonel Francis E. Heath

According to Colonel Heath, General Humphreys himself ordered the men of the 19th Maine to stop his own men from retreating with bayonets, but Heath refused to obey the order.[80] Instead, he ordered his men to lie down to let the 3rd Corps men pass through the line. Then, rising as one, the 400 men of the 19th Maine poured a withering fire into Lang's Florida brigade (and probably the right flank of Confederate General Wright's brigade). To its left, the 1st Minnesota had been ordered personally by General Hancock to stop the charge of Wilcox's Alabamians, which it did temporarily, losing over 80% of its men. However, this sacrifice allowed General Hancock time to bring up reinforcements to plug the gap.

As Lang's brigade retreated, Lieutenant Colonel Henry W. Cunningham of Belfast reported movement to the right. Colonel Heath ordered the regiment back about twenty-five paces to get out of the smoke of battle and found that this report was not correct. He then gave the order to fix bayonets and charge the enemy remaining at the regiment's front. The rebels fell back as the regiment advanced almost to the Emmitsburg Road, capturing many prisoners, several battle flags, and recovering cannon that had been abandoned by the 5th U.S. Battery. As they returned to their original line to the cheers of troops on Cemetery Ridge, the men of the 19th Maine were dismayed to find that several of the battle trophies that had been rightly won were now in the possession of men from a New York regiment that had not participated in the charge. Sergeant Silas Adams of Bowdoinham later wrote, "the honor of capturing the 8th Florida flag went to Sergeant Hogan of the Seventy-second New York of the Excelsior Brigade. When Hogan picked up the flag in question there was not a live Rebel soldier within a half a mile of him unless such Rebel soldier was a prisoner of war."[81]

The triumph of the 19th Maine came at a heavy price; over 130 men of the regiment were killed or wounded on July 2. That evening the regiment stayed on Cemetery Ridge to await developments on the following day, when they again would be asked to repel a rebel charge.

No Higher Valor
Maine Medal of Honor Recipients for Actions at Gettysburg

NAME	RANK	BIRTHPLACE	REGIMENT
Joshua L. Chamberlain	Colonel	Brewer	20th Maine
William B. Hincks	Sergeant Major	Bucksport	14th Connecticut
Henry D. O'Brien	Corporal	Calais	1st Minnesota
James Richmond	Private	Unknown	8th Ohio
Andrew Tozier	Sergeant	Monmouth	20th Maine

Maine Veterans of Gettysburg Who Received the Medal of Honor for Other Actions During the Civil War

NAME	RANK	BIRTHPLACE	UNIT	BATTLE
Adelbert Ames	1st Lt.	Rockland	5th U.S. Artillery	First Bull Run
Robert Boody	Sergeant	Limington	40th New York	Williamsburg & Chancellorsville
Charles Clark	1st Lt.	Sangerville	6th Maine	Brooks Ford
John F. Chase	Private	Chelsea	5th Maine	Chancellorsville
Albert E. Fernald	1st Lt.	Winterport	20th Maine	Five Forks
Moses C. Hanscom	Corporal	Danville	19th Maine	Bristoe Station
Ephraim W. Harrington	Sergeant	Waterford	2nd Vermont	Fredericksburg
Oliver O. Howard	Brig. Gen.	Leeds	61st New York	Fair Oaks
Charles Mattocks	Major	Danille, VT (lived in Portland when he enlisted)	17th Maine	Sailor's Creek
Walter G. Morrill	Captain	Williamsburg	20th Maine	Rappahannock Station
Otis O. Roberts	Sergeant	Sangerville	6th Maine	Rappahannock Station
Charles H. Smith	Colonel	Hollis	1st Maine Cavalry	St. Mary's Church
Sydney W. Thaxter	Major	Bangor	1st Maine Cavalry	Hatcher's Run
Edward N. Whittier	1st Lt.	Portland	5th Maine Battery	Fisher's Hill

Ninety Men from Maine were awarded the Medal of Honor for actions during the Civil War. Go to www.history.army.mil/moh/ for a complete list of Medal of Honor winners and their citations.

"AS IF A VOLCANO HAD BEEN LET LOOSE"
Stevens's 5th Maine Battery — *July 2, 1863, 4:00-8:30 p.m.*

Having barely escaped capture on Seminary Ridge on July 1, the 5th Maine Battery was comfortably situated behind earthworks as day broke on July 2 on a small knoll to the west of and attached to Culp's Hill. From this position the battery had a clear field of fire across the slope of Cemetery Hill down to the Town of Gettysburg. However, the openness of this position made the battery a target of Confederate sharpshooters concealed in bushes and behind fences along the banks of Rock Creek. In the early afternoon, one of these sharpshooters targeted Captain Stevens, shooting him through both legs below the knee.[82] As he was removed from the field, Lieutenant Edward N. Whittier of Gorham took command of the battery.

Taking advantage of a lull in the fighting at this portion of the field, the remaining officers of the battery used the time to take sightings using a French "ordnance glass" to determine the range of various positions across the field. They then fired some shots of various types of shell to correct for elevation and fuse length. In this way, when the time came to go into action, the battery would be deadly accurate in its fire.

Private John Chase — Did We Win the Battle?

The angel of death had a hard time collecting Private John F. Chase of Augusta, Maine, a member of the 5th Maine Battery. Hit by shrapnel while in action on what is now called Stevens's Knoll during the second day of the Battle of Gettysburg, he suffered a horrible wound to his right arm, lost his left eye, and sustained forty-eight other wounds to his face and chest. In the heat of battle he was carried to the rear and left for dead. There he lay on the field for two days, much of the time in a pouring rain, until a burial party found him and discovered that he was still breathing. "Did we win the battle?" were his first words after regaining consciousness, according to newspaper accounts.

In the days following, J. O. Sloan, a chaplain at Gettysburg, visited Private Chase in an outlying barn that was serving as a field hospital. His right arm had been amputated just above the elbow. "He was indeed a pitiful sight," Sloan reported. "The surgeon said there was no hope for him; he could not live but a day or two. He was carried out of the hospital and put in a tent alone; there to die." But his Maine stubbornness took over, his condition improved and he was transferred to the Seminary Hospital. There his condition suddenly worsened. After three weeks the doctors determined that he would die at any moment. In order to give his bed to a more promising patient, he was again taken outside to a tent to die. Guess what? He did die . . . fifty-one years later in 1914.

Private Chase returned to Augusta, got married, and fathered five children. He held several U.S. Patents, including one for a collapsible hoop skirt, and moved to St. Petersburg, Florida, where he was involved in several successful business ventures. In 1888, he was awarded the Medal of Honor for actions at the Battle of Chancellorsville. In 2009, his descendants donated the medal to the Chancellorsville Visitor's Center of the Fredericksburg and Spotsylvania National Military Park, where it can be seen on exhibit today.

Around 4:00 p.m., in support of General Longstreet's attack at the southern end of the battlefield, General Ewell ordered his artillery to attack positions on Cemetery and Culp's Hills. Confederate Major Joseph Latimer, not yet twenty years old and known as the "Boy Major," moved his fourteen gun artillery battalion, as if on parade, to Benner's Hill, a position about 1,400 yards to the northeast of Cemetery Hill, and began a long-range duel with the Federal artillery. The 5th Maine replied along with other artillery units on Cemetery Hill. As Benner's Hill was extremely open and exposed, Latimer's guns were silenced within an hour. Latimer was severely wounded in this exchange and died after complications of an arm amputation on August 1, 1863.

Finding that the battery ammunition was running low, Lieutenant Whittier had all that was left in caissons transferred to the limber-chests and sent the caissons back to the supply train about two miles to the rear. At about 7:45 p.m., a lookout shouted, "Look at those men!" He had spotted Hoke's Brigade of North Carolinians (now led by Colonel Isaac Avery) and Hays' Brigade (the famous Louisiana Tigers) as they aligned to attack Union positions on East Cemetery Hill from the town of Gettysburg. As the Confederate forces had to first march southeast then turn right to attack the men on Cemetery Hill, they first presented their front then left flank to artillery fire from the 5th Maine battery.

Lieutenant Whittier in his report in Maine at Gettysburg wrote of this moment:

> All comrades of the old Fifth know how quickly and how well our guns opened the artillery fire that evening, for the order, "Case 2 ½ degrees, 3 seconds time," had barely been heard before up went the lids of the limber-chests, the fuses were cut in another moment, and the guns were loaded as if on drill. Slap went the heads of the rammers against the faces of the pieces, a most welcome sound, for at the same moment came the order, "Fire by battery," and at once there was the flash and roar of our six guns.[83]

Colonel Adin Underwood of the 33rd Massachusetts (11th Corps) posted in the valley below later wrote to Lieutenant Whittier, "right over my head, it seemed to me, there was a flash of light, a roar and a crash as if a volcano had been let loose."[84] As the Confederate line moved up toward Cemetery Hill, the artillery posted there was unable to depress their guns without hitting Union troops in front of them. However, the 5th Maine Battery was in perfect position to continue to hit the enemy as they charged. Lieutenant Whittier moved the right two guns of the battery back and to the left as their field of fire decreased. They continued firing even as it got darker by using the fire of Confederate rifles as aiming points. Running out of shells, the battery began using canister at long range.

While some of the charging Confederates did reach the crest of Cemetery Hill, they were soon overwhelmed by Federal reinforcements. The combined effect of artillery fire and rifle fire had caused too many casualties to carry the position. By 9:00 p.m. the fight was over. Lieutenant Whittier, out of ammunition, moved the battery to the rear near the Baltimore Pike, to allow infantry to move into his position on Culp's Hill. However, once there the caissons returned with a new supply of ammunition. So Whittier moved the battery back in position, removing the infantry that had taken their comfortable spot behind earthworks. By 10:30 pm, the 5th Maine Battery was right back where it started the day, having suffered only a couple of casualties and four horses killed. The battery was not actively engaged during the fight on July 3, but stayed in position on a spot now known as "Stevens's Knoll."

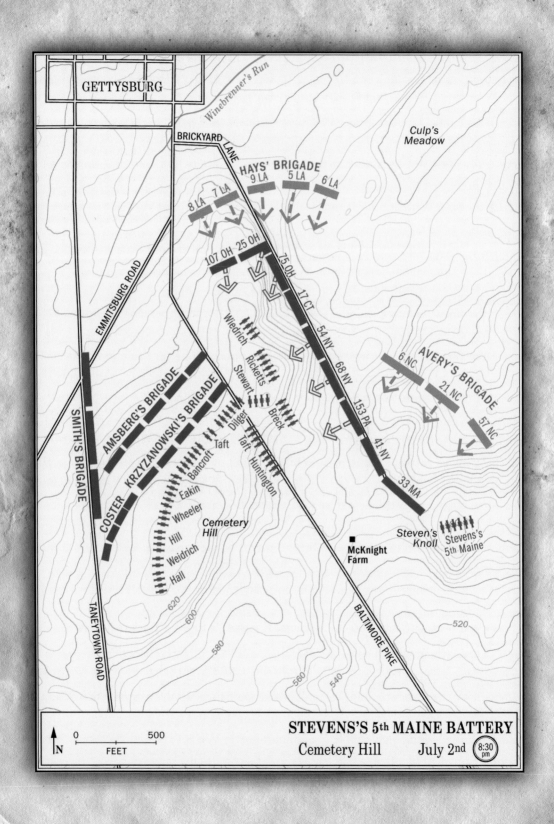

GETTYSBURG

Winebrenner's Run

Culp's Meadow

BRICKYARD LANE

HAYS' BRIGADE
9 LA   5 LA   6 LA

8 LA   7 LA

EMMITSBURG ROAD

107 OH   25 OH

25 OH

17 CT

Wiedrich

54 NY

Ricketts

AVERY'S BRIGADE
6 NC

68 NY

Stewart

21 NC

AMSBERG'S BRIGADE

Breck

153 PA

57 NC

KRZYZANOWSKI'S BRIGADE

41 NY

SMITH'S BRIGADE

Dilger

COSTER

Bancroft

Taft

Taft Huntington

33 MA

Eakin

Wheeler

Cemetery Hill

McKnight Farm

Steven's Knoll

Stevens's 5th Maine

Hill

Weidrich

Hall

620

600

580

560

540

520

BALTIMORE PIKE

TANEYTOWN ROAD

0   500
FEET
N

STEVENS'S 5th MAINE BATTERY
Cemetery Hill   July 2nd   8:30 pm

Albion Parris Howe — Dashing Readiness

Born in Standish, Maine, Albion P. Howe graduated 8th in his class at the West Point Military Academy (18 spots ahead of John Reynolds). He served in the Mexican War under General Winfield Scott and taught mathematics at West Point for three years. He served under Colonel Robert E. Lee during the suppression and capture of John Brown at Harper's Ferry in 1859. At the Battle of Malvern Hill he received the brevet rank of major in the regular army and became a Brigadier General in the volunteer service in June of 1862.

Following the Battle of Antietam he was promoted to the command of the Second Division of the 6th Corps. At Gettysburg, his division was the last one to reach the battlefield and was held in reserve. The two brigades of his command were assigned to opposite ends of the battlefield, leaving him with without much to do. The best that can be said about his service during the battle can be found in his own official report written in August of 1863. "The dashing readiness with which the division went on to the field on the evening of the 2d, after its long and continuous march of the previous day and night, and the handsome manner in which it bore itself during the engagement, were worthy of its former reputation."*

Due to bad relations with his corps commander, General John Sedgwick, Howe was relieved of his command. Following the war, he served on the Lincoln funeral honor guard and was a member of the military commission that tried the Lincoln conspirators. He was not one of the five commissioners who petitioned President Johnson to commute the sentence of Mary Surratt. He died in 1897 and is buried in Cambridge, Massachusetts.

* **The War of the Rebellion: a Compilation of the Official Records of the Union and Confederate Armies, Government Printing Office, Series I, Volume XXVII/1, page 675.**

NOTES

29. Hood, John Bell, *Advance and Retreat* (Reprint, Blue and Grey Press, 1985). page 57.

30. Cadmus M. Wilcox in the *National Tribune* (Washington, D.C.), May 16, 1885.

31. At that moment, this turned out to be an incorrect assumption. The three Confederate regiments on the other side of Pitzer's Woods were actually part of General Hill's 3rd Corps, the 8th, 10th, and 11th Alabama under the command of Brigadier General Cadmus M. Wilcox, who were simply attempting to extend the Confederate line along Seminary Ridge. The actual flanking maneuver of Longstreet's two divisions had barely begun by noon of July 2.

32. Trudeau, Noah Andre, *Gettysburg, a Testing of Courage* (New York, 2002), page 326.

33. Almost as soon as the battle of Gettysburg was over, the controversy over General

Sickles's actions on the second day began. It continues to this day. His supporters claim that if he had maintained his original position on the low slope of Cemetery Ridge, Longstreet's men would have encountered little opposition as they crossed the Emmitsburg Road, allowing them to attack the Union line much sooner in the day. In addition, the capture of Big and Little Round Top by Confederate troops would probably have occurred. As these commanded the surrounding area, this may have forced General Meade to abandon the field. Thus, it was aggressive tactics (and pure fortune) to be able to meet Longstreet's attack earlier in an advanced position. However, it cannot be ignored that Sickles's foolish move endangered the entire army and resulted in the almost total sacrifice and wrecking of the 3rd Corps — it would not take the field again as a corps in the Union army after the battle at Gettysburg.

34. While Berdan could claim some credit for taking this idea to the War Department, it was not an original concept. Many historians believe that the real credit should go to Casper Trepp, a native of Switzerland and a veteran of the Crimean War, who came to America and persuaded Berdan, who had much more clout, to go the War Department with the idea. Trepp served as a captain in the 1st U.S. Sharpshooters.

35. Christian Sharps' rifle design owed much to an earlier breech loading rifle patented in 1811 by John Hancock Hall of Portland, Maine.

36. For those having trouble picturing how the pellet primer system worked, think of the PEZ candy dispenser. Many users of the Sharps rifle did not trust this system and continued to use individual percussion caps in combat.

37. The reader might wonder why the entire Union Army was not issued this weapon, given its great advantages over breech loaders. Due to its complex design, the Sharps rifle cost about three times as much to produce (about $60) as the most popular rifle of the Civil War, the Springfield rifle. In addition, many of the higher ups in the War Department, including General Winfield Scott, worried that the men would needlessly waste ammunition and not take time to aim if they could fire so many rounds in a minute. So only about 11 thousand of the 1859 model Sharps rifles were produced, as opposed to the one million 1861 Springfields sold to the army during the war.

38. Dalton, Peter, ed. *Soldiers in Green: The Civil War Diaries of James Mero Matthews, 2nd U. S. Sharpshooters,* (Sandy Point, ME: Richardson's Civil War Roundtable, 2002), pages 28-29.

39. Dalton, pages 170-171.

40. Dalton, page 159.

41. Stoughton is often referred to in several histories of the battle as Lt. Colonel

Stoughton. Although he was promoted after the battle, backdated to June 24th, at the Battle of Gettysburg he still held the rank of Major.

42. The exact placement of the eight companies of the 2nd U.S. Sharpshooters along an approximately 1,000-foot-long line was probably — from left to right – B-F-H-C-G-E-A-D.

43. Quoted in Orr, Timothy. " 'On Such Slender Threads does the Fate of Nations Depend': The Second United States Sharpshooters Defend the Union Left on July Second," in "The Most Shocking Battle I Ever Witnessed": The Second Day at Gettysburg (Published by Gettysburg National Military Park, 2008): page 132.

44. Dalton, pages 160-161.

45. *Maine at Gettysburg*, page 352.

46. Again, a key moment in the battle. Had these 22 men been with the 15th Alabama during its subsequent attack on the 20th Maine regiment on Little Round Top, the full strength Alabama regiment may have been able to flank the Union position (and perhaps Colonel Joshua Chamberlain would have spent the rest of the war in Libby Prison).

47. The list of Company D's casualties at Gettysburg – Captain Jacob McClure (w), Sergeant Josiah Gray (k), Sergeant John Wade (w), Corporal Argyl Morse (prisoner), Corporal John Rounds (p), Corporal Richard Boynton (p), Private John Allen (w), Private James Bradbury (w), Private Francis Ladd (p), Private James Pendleton (w) and Private Charles Wentworth (missing).

48. Quoted in Orr, page 142.

49. Gould, Edward K., *Major-General Hiram G. Berry* (Rockland, Maine, 1899), page 44. The flag had the phrase "From the Home of Knox" on it, in honor of General Henry Knox, the famous Revolutionary War hero and first Secretary of War.

50. Colonel Hiram Berry was promoted to brigade command in March of 1862 and eventually became a Major General in command of a division. He was killed by a sharpshooters bullet at the Battle of Chancellorsville while trying to rally his men.

51. The original of the name "Devil's Den" is uncertain, it was not in common use until after the battle, although some resident's claim that it got its name in the 1850's when a large fifteen-foot foot black snake was reported in the area.

52. It was probably a shot from Smith's Battery that resulted in the wounding of Confederate General John B. Hood.

53. Elijah Walker to John Bachelder, January 5, 1885, Bacheldor Papers, New Hampshire Historical Society.

54. *Maine at Gettysburg*, page 182.

55. Pullen, John J., *The Twentieth Maine* (Philadelphia, 1957), page 36.

56. After the Battle of Gettysburg, the men of the 20th Maine presented their battle flag to Ames, in recognition of the excellent training they received while under his command.

57. *Maine at Gettysburg*, page 276.

58. Pullen, page 110.

59. Ibid., page 111.

60. Not only had Colonel Oates sent off about twenty men with canteens to find water, he had also detached his Company A to capture a wagon train to the right that he had viewed from Big Round Top. Thus, at a crucial time in the battle, he had sent away about ten percent of his regiment, men he could have used in his fight with the 20th Maine.

61. Chamberlain kept the revolver as a souvenir of the war, and delighted in recounting the tale of its acquisition to any visitors. The actual revolver is in the collection of the Maine State Museum in Augusta. An exact replica of the pistol is currently on display in the Chamberlain Museum library in Brunswick, Maine. Chamberlain was actually wounded twice during this encounter. One bullet had sliced the instep of his boot causing him to limp, while another had hit his sword scabbard, bending it back and causing a bad bruise. Unknown at the time, Chamberlain had escaped death when a Confederate sharpshooter, who had Chamberlain in his sights, for a reason he could not explain, could not pull the trigger. Years later he wrote to Chamberlain saying he was glad that he had not fired and hoped Chamberlain was glad too. (found in Pullen, page 122).

62. Two men in the 20th Maine were awarded the Medal of Honor for actions on Little Round Top. Chamberlain received his medal in 1893. This original medal was lost, and later rediscovered in 2013, and donated to the Pejebscot Historical Society in Brunswick, Maine. Sergeant Andrew J. Tozier of Plymouth received his medal in 1898. His citation read, "At the crisis of the engagement this soldier, a color bearer, stood alone in an advanced position, the regiment having been borne back, and defended his colors with musket and ammunition picked up at his feet." Chamberlain granted one battlefield promotion on Little Round Top. Private George Washington Buck of Linneus in Aroostook County had been unjustly demoted to private in a dispute with the quartermaster. Colonel Chamberlain found him lying on the slope of Little Round Top mortally wounded by a shot to the chest. Chamberlain told him he was promoting him back to sergeant on the spot. Taken to the rear, soon afterwards Buck died, to be buried in an unknown grave somewhere on the battlefield.

63. The enthusiasm with which the recruits enlisted was due partly to the generous bounty provided by the U.S. Government and the State of Maine. In addition to the $140 paid upon enlistment ($127 plus a month's pay), the recruit would receive $75 and 160 acres of Federal land upon being mustered out.

64. Colonel de Trobriand was an interesting character. A French aristocrat, lawyer, poet, and novelist, he emigrated at a young age to the United States. An expert swordsman who had fought several duels, de Trobriand married a New York socialite and became a naturalized U.S. citizen. He was very popular with his men, who took to calling him "Colonel Froggy." After the war he wrote a book about his experiences, Four Years with the Army of the Potomac.

65. It should be noted here that the officers of the 17th Maine were divided on who should take command after Colonel Roberts' departure. Many of them preferred Major West for command. In fact, 21 officers in the regiment signed a letter to Governor Coburn demanding the West be appointed to command to the point of accusing Lt. Colonel Merrill of cowardice at the Battle of Chancellorsville. Much of this was due to the desire of Major West to take command of the regiment. However, after Merrill's conspicuous actions and courage at the Battle of Gettysburg, the issue became moot for a while. However, in October of 1863, West took command of the regiment. The West-Merrill feud would continue to the end of their lives.

66. *Maine at Gettysburg,* page 198.

67. Ibid.

68. In a letter from Lt. Colonel Charles Merrill to Captain Ben M. Pratt, Assistant Adjutant General, July 5, 1863, Maine State Archives.

69. *Maine at Gettysburg,* page 132.

70. In a letter from Colonel Moses Lakeman to Adjutant General John L. Hodsdon, July 13, 1863, Maine State Archives.

71. Lemke, William, *A Pride of Lions* (Massachusetts, 1997), page 197.

72. The artillery battery in the American Civil War usually was officered by a captain, three lieutenants, and 150 men with 6 guns and 88 horses.

73. Baker, Levi W., *History of the Ninth Mass. Battery,* (1888), pages 41-42.

74. *Maine at Gettysburg,* page 328.

75. *Maine at Gettysburg,* page 312.

76. Smith, John Day, *The History of the Nineteenth Regiment of Maine Volunteer Infantry* (Minneapolis, 1909), pages 41-42. Smith eventually became a judge in Minnesota, thus his book was published there.

77. Ibid., pages 56-57. One wonders if it was not Private John Day Smith who fell in the ditch.

78. Ibid., page 70.

79. The oldest regular army unit still on active duty, the 5th Artillery Battery was originally led by Alexander Hamilton during the American Revolution.

80. Many dispute Colonel Heath's story about General Humphreys and his order, including the regimental historian. In his original account of the engagement, Colonel Heath had written that he received the order from an officer that he "supposed" was General Humphreys.

81. Smith, page 72.

82. Stevens would return to service in 1863 and remain until the end of the war. After the war, he was elected to the State Legislature, served on the Maine Battlefield Commission and became a sheriff and probate judge. He died in 1918, at the ripe age of 87.

83. *Maine at Gettysburg*, page 94-95.

84. Ibid., page 95.

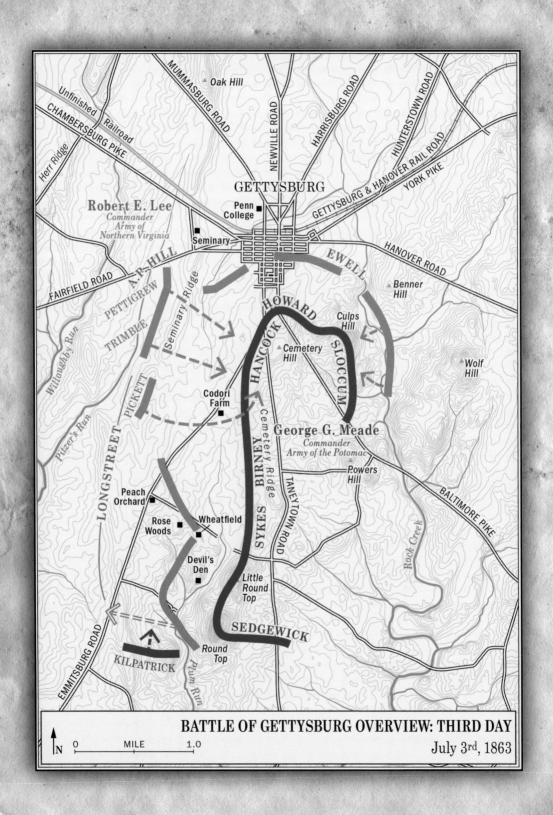

BATTLE OF GETTYSBURG OVERVIEW: THIRD DAY
July 3rd, 1863

N
0   MILE   1.0

DAY THREE
July 3, 1863

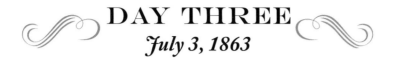

As night fell on the field at Gettysburg after the second day of fighting, the corps commanders of the Army of the Potomac met at General Meade's headquarters to discuss the situation and decide a course of action. Most agreed to remain in a defensive position to await any further attacks. As the meeting broke up, General Meade predicted to one of his generals that the next attack would come at the center of the line on Cemetery Ridge. He also decided to keep the 14,000 men of the 6th Corps under General Sedgwick in reserve in case of a Confederate breakthrough.

General Lee had also decided to stay. On July 2, his army had advanced and fought well, actually inflicting more casualties on the Union army than his army had received (one of the few times in the war that the offensive force lost less than the defensive force). However, General Longstreet's attacks had not taken any strategic ground, falling short of capturing either of the Round Top hills or Cemetery Ridge. The Union Army still held the high ground.

Lee's plan for July 3 was indeed to attack the center of the Union line at Cemetery Ridge. For this effort he had the fresh division of Longstreet's Corps commanded by Major General George Pickett. He also finally had Major General J. E. B. Stuart's Cavalry Corps on hand to create panic at the rear of the Federal line. Prior to the attack, General Lee intended to collect all of the artillery of the Army of Northern Virginia (about 160 pieces) to fire at the Union line in the greatest bombardment ever heard in America in order to clear the way for Pickett's men.

However, Pickett's division was not enough to do the job, and the rest of Longstreet's men were used up. So General Lee added several elements from Hill's 3rd Corps, making a total striking force of about 12,500 men. At about 1:00 p.m. the bombardment commenced. Dr. Jacobs at Pennsylvania College recorded a temperature of about 87 degrees. It was going to be a hot day. Near the center of the Union line, very close to a copse of trees that became the Confederate aiming point, the 19th Maine Regiment waited. A few miles further east, the 1st Maine Cavalry, posted along the Hanover Road, also waited for General Stuart's attack.

By 5:00 p.m., it was all over. Pickett's Charge became immortalized, but the end result was an additional 7,000 casualties. General Stuart's exhausted men could not break through the strong Union cavalry position on the Hanover Road. As the men limped back to Seminary Ridge, General Lee said to one of his generals, "It is all my fault — you must help me out the best way you can." As the Confederate Army retreated back to Virginia, it brought along a seventeen-mile-long wagon train of wounded and dying soldiers.[85]

"WE FELT LIKE WE WERE EQUAL TO IT"
19th Maine Regiment — *July 3, 1863, 1:00 — 4:00 p.m.*

As the day began on Friday, July 3, 1863, four companies (B, D, E, and F) of the 19th Maine were moved forward of the Union line on Cemetery Ridge to act as skirmishers under the command of Captain Folger. Posted very close to the Emmitsburg Road, near the Codori farm, these men had to stay close to the ground to avoid the fire of Confederate sharpshooters. Most of the men had not had time to have breakfast and, in fact, had not had anything to eat for over twenty-four hours. There was also no chance to draw water anywhere as they concealed themselves in the grass.

The rest of the regiment remained up on the ridge about 400 yards behind the skirmish line. On the regiment's right, the 82nd New York and 20th Massachusetts were posted. On the left, the remainder of the 1st Minnesota and 15th Massachusetts took position behind the hastily constructed small wall of stones and rails that extended along the line. The day became very hot with scarcely a breath of a breeze as the men waited. Doubtless some hoped that General Lee and his army had had enough and as the day wore on to 10:00 a.m., 11:00 a.m., then noon, it seemed as if this was the case.

Then about three quarters of a mile to the west, Confederate artillery began appearing in the open field. Not just some of the Confederate artillery, almost all of it . . . more than 160 guns. At 1:00 p.m. two Confederate guns fired a signal round. What followed was the greatest cannonade in history up to that moment. No army anywhere in the world had ever faced anything like it. It was a sound that broke windows in Gettysburg, it was a sound that carried all the way to Pittsburgh, over 180 miles away, and it seemed to the men of the 19th Maine that it was all aimed at them.

Fortunately, the Confederate artillerymen were firing a little high as a large percentage of the shells exploded to the rear, killing a lot of horses and breaking up supply wagons. In fact, the safest men on the field were probably the four companies of the 19th Maine posted forward as skirmishers. Finally, after about two hours, the Union artillery began to slacken fire and pull back, with the hope that this movement would deceive the Confederates into thinking that their fire was effective. It worked. Then the cry, "Here

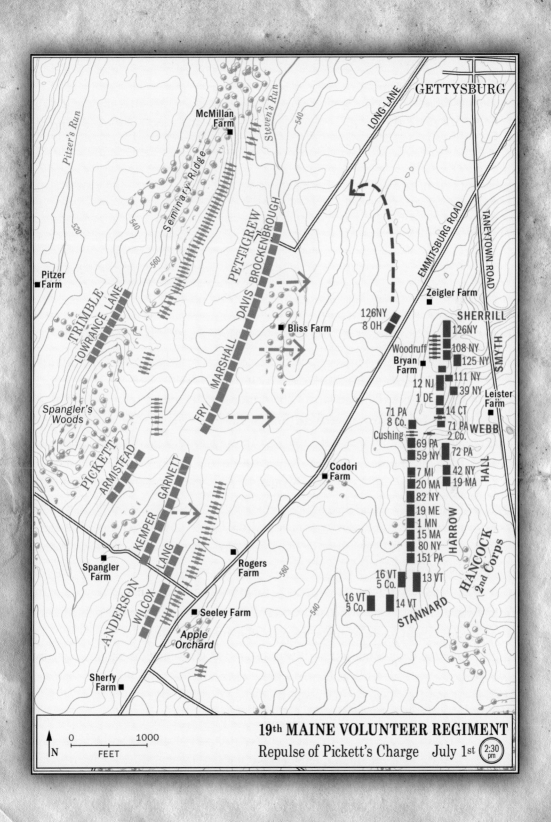

GETTYSBURG

Pitzer's Run

McMillan Farm

Steven's Run

540

LONG LANE

EMMITSBURG ROAD

TANEYTOWN ROAD

520

Seminary Ridge

560

PETTIGREW

BROCKENBROUGH

Pitzer Farm

TRIMBLE

LOWRANCE LANE

DAVIS

MARSHALL

Bliss Farm

Zeigler Farm

126NY
8 OH

SHERRILL

126NY

108 NY

SMYTH

Woodruff
Bryan
Farm

125 NY

111 NY

39 NY

Leister
Farm

540

560

FRY

12 NJ
1 DE

14 CT

Spangler's
Woods

71 PA
8 Co.

71 PA
2 Co.

WEBB

Cushing

PICKETT

ARMISTEAD

GARNETT

Codori
Farm

69 PA
59 NY

72 PA

7 MI

42 NY

20 MA

19 MA

HALL

82 NY

Spangler
Farm

KEMPER

LANG

Rogers
Farm

19 ME

1 MN

15 MA

80 NY

HARROW

HANCOCK
2nd Corps

151 PA

ANDERSON

WILCOX

Seeley Farm

560

16 VT
5 Co.

13 VT

Apple
Orchard

16 VT
5 Co.

14 VT

540

STANNARD

Sherfy
Farm

19th MAINE VOLUNTEER REGIMENT

Repulse of Pickett's Charge   July 1st   2:30 pm

N   0   1000
     FEET

comes the infantry," as the mile long line of Confederate soldiers appeared from the woods on Seminary Ridge.

Relieved that the cannonade was over, the men of the Union Army on Cemetery Ridge looked on in awe and admiration at the spectacle, as the Confederate line moved forward in perfect parade ground fashion, regimental flags flying. "We knew then that a decisive moment was coming; and we

View of a copse of trees from the 19th Maine monument

felt we were equal to it," said an officer of the 19th Maine, as, years afterward, he described the scenes of the hour.[86] The men in the skirmish line moved back as the rebels advanced (some of them actually moved to the left and joined in with the Vermont brigade of General George Stannard). The Union artillery then returned to the field and immediately began firing shells at the Confederate line. To the South, Freeman McGilvery's concealed batteries fired destructive enfilading solid shot and shrapnel at the southern flank.

To add to the Confederate woes, the men of Pickett's division had to oblique to the left to close the gap between themselves and the 3rd Corps divisions of Pettigrew and Trimble, thus also exposing their flank as they approached the Union line. When the Confederates approached to within 400 yards, the Union line let loose a tremendous volley. Stannards Vermonters (along with some Maine men) pushed out in front of the line, turned right, and fired into the flank of Confederate General Kemper's brigade, which also received fire from the 19th Maine as it passed in front. At the copse of trees, the Union line was broken, but the men to the left rushed up to restore the line, including the 19th Maine.

At this point the battle became a wild melee of close quarter fighting, pushing, and shoving. Colonel Heath was hit by a piece of shell in the shoulder (just moments after General Hancock received his wound) and command of the 19th Maine fell to Lt. Colonel Henry W. Cunningham of Belfast. Positioned now just south of the copse of trees, the 19th Maine and the 20th Massachusetts moved along the space between the trees and the wall to cut off those Confederates that had broken the line. For about ten minutes, the men mingled with the enemy, using rifle butts and firing over the heads of those in front (even throwing stones), forcing the 300 or so rebel soldiers to surrender. The line was saved, Pickett's Charge was over, Lee's great gamble had failed.[87]

"THOSE MAINE MEN WOULD CHARGE STRAIGHT INTO HELL IF ORDERED TO."
1st Maine Cavalry — *July 3, 1863, 2:15 — 5:30 p.m.*

No Union cavalry regiment participated in more battles during the Civil War than the 1st Maine Cavalry. Third-five different major engagements were borne upon the flag of the regiment. It was once estimated that the 1st Maine Cavalry came under fire at more than one hundred different places during the war. It suffered more men killed in action and dead from wounds than any other cavalry unit of the war. Of the 3,226 men who at one time or another served with the 1st Maine, 518 of them died in the service of their country, with an additional 145 men captured and held in Confederate prisons until their release.[88]

Organized in the fall of 1861, the regiment was made up of twelve companies with a total of 49 officers and 1,109 enlisted men under the command of Colonel John Goddard of Cape Elizabeth. The men came from every section of the state. They went into camp at the State Fairgrounds in Augusta, which was soon named Camp Penobscot, setting up a tent city and awaiting orders. However, it did not seem that the war department knew what they wanted to do with these cavalrymen. For a while, it was thought that the 1st Maine Cavalry would go with General Butler on his expedition to Louisiana, but nothing came of that. So the regiment stayed in camp during the entire winter of 1861-62, losing about 200 men to illness and exposure during that hard Maine season.

The regiment finally made it to Washington, D.C., in March of 1862. For its first year of service the 1st Maine was divided and sent to various places in Virginia and Maryland. Five companies served at Harper's Ferry for a while, scouting and guarding the railroads there. The other seven companies held various positions along the Rappahannock River, getting as far south as Culpepper Court House on one occasion, taking part in the Battle of Cedar Mountain, and being involved in the retreat from the Battle of Second Bull Run.

During the winter of 1862-1863, the Union cavalry was reorganized into a Cavalry Corps and the separate companies of the 1st Maine finally came together again as one unit in the 1st Brigade of the 3rd Division, under the command of Colonel Calvin S. Douty of Dover. During the spring campaign of 1863, the regiment participated in Stoneman's Raid during the Chancellorsville campaign, suffering more than thirty casualties.

The Gettysburg campaign actually started with the Union cavalry's surprise attack at Brandy Station on June 9, 1863. Here the 1st Maine Cavalry participated in its first grand charge. Drawing sabers, the regiment charged some artillery, then pushed the Confederate cavalry back about a mile before stopping. General Kilpatrick later stated that it was "one of the best charges ever made and saved not only the brigade but the whole division in this action."[89] While the battle ended in a draw with the Union troopers

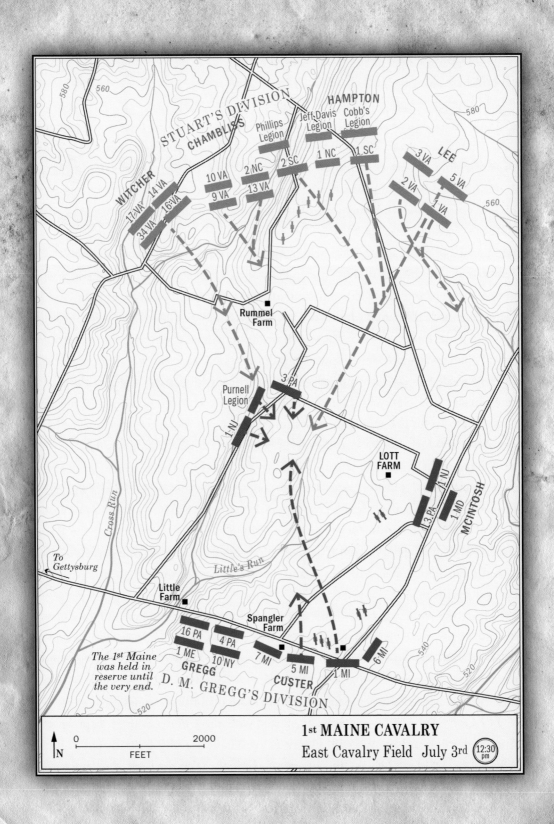

STUART'S DIVISION
CHAMBLISS

HAMPTON

LEE

WITCHER

Phillips Legion

Jeff Davis Legion

Cobb's Legion

10 VA

2 NC

2 SC

1 NC

1 SC

3 VA

5 VA

17 VA

14 VA

9 VA

13 VA

2 VA

1 VA

34 VA

16 VA

580

560

580

560

Rummel Farm

3 PA

Purnell Legion

LOTT FARM

1 NJ

1 NJ

3 PA

1 MD

McINTOSH

Cross Run

To Gettysburg

Little's Run

Little Farm

Spangler Farm

16 PA

4 PA

6 MI

The 1st Maine was held in reserve until the very end.

1 ME

10 NY

7 MI

5 MI

1 MI

GREGG

CUSTER

D. M. GREGG'S DIVISION

520

540

520

520

1st **MAINE CAVALRY**

East Cavalry Field   July 3rd

12:30 pm

N

0   2000

FEET

retreating back across the Rappahannock River, it was the first time they had stood up to J.E.B Stuart's cavalry.

On June 17, the 1st Maine Cavalry, after riding twenty miles, participated in a cavalry fight at Aldie, Virginia. Here companies D and H charged a stone wall, capturing that position. During this brief action, Colonel Douty and Captain George J. Summat were killed and Captain William Montgomery of Orland was wounded. Lt. Colonel Charles H. Smith of Eastport then was promoted to Colonel and given command of the regiment. This was followed by more fighting at Middleburg on June 19 and Upperville on June 21. At the later engagement, Colonel Smith was ordered by General Kilpatrick (nicknamed "Kill-Cavalry" for his habit of ordering desperate charges) to charge through the town and drive out the enemy. As the men prepared

Colonel Charles H. Smith

for the charge, Kilpatrick was heard to say, "That First Maine would charge straight into hell if it were ordered to."[90] During this brief fight Captain Andrew B. Spurling of Orland was wounded.

Having been in the saddle for most of the month of June, the 1st Maine Cavalry arrived at Gettysburg at daybreak on July 2 with only 396 men and 23 officers on the rolls. During the day, the regiment participated in some small skirmishes but went into bivouac that evening near the Baltimore Pike having seen very little action. The next day the 1st Maine moved east to the Hanover Road and stayed there in reserve.

As in most cavalry fights, the Gettysburg cavalry battle was a confused mess of charges and counter-charges over a large field. General Stuart hoped to break through the Federal cavalry screen to attack the rear of the Army of the Potomac just as Pickett's Charge commenced. However, with the advantage and inspiration of men fighting on their home ground, the Union cavalry, led by General David M. Gregg and newly commissioned General George Armstrong Custer, stopped the formerly superior Confederate cavalry and pushed them back to their starting point. In his expansive *History of the 1st Maine Cavalry*, historian Edward Tobie summed up the importance of this cavalry battle:

"This engagement goes down to history as one of the finest cavalry fights of the war, and one most important in its results; for had the enemy succeeded in getting in the rear of the Union forces, that day would have resulted differently, and the name of Gettysburg would suggest a state of affairs which it is not agreeable to contemplate."[91]

The 1st Maine Cavalry was only lightly engaged near the end of the fight on the cavalry field. Following the Battle of Gettysburg, the regiment pursued the retreating Confederate Army as it moved back to Virginia, capturing many prisoners, including a large section of the rebels' wagon train loaded with wounded soldiers.

Henry D. O'Brien — "Characteristic Impetuosity"

The 1st Minnesota Regiment was made up entirely of men from other parts of the United States and Europe. There were no native Minnesotans who fought in the Civil War because the area had not become a state until 1858. At least a hundred men in the regiment were Maine born or raised. One of them, Henry D. O'Brien, born in Calais, Maine in 1842, was awarded the Medal of Honor for bravery at the Battle of Gettysburg.

Slightly wounded in the side during the gallant charge of the regiment on July 2, Corporal O'Brien carried a badly wounded friend, Ernest Jefferson, to safety. He returned to the regiment to participate in the battle on July 3. On the Union line on Cemetery Ridge to the immediate left flank of the 19th Maine, the 1st Minnesota soon came into contact with troops from Confederate General Kemper's brigade. The regimental color bearer, Corporal John Dehn, was shot in the hand, breaking the staff of the flag. O'Brien picked up the flag, "with his characteristic impetuosity sprang with it towards the enemy on the first sound of the word "Charge," and kept it noticeably in advance of every other color in the rush then made . . . which every man of the First Minnesota ran forward to protect."* O'Brien was again wounded during this fight. The regiment captured many Confederate soldiers and one battle flag.

In 1864, Lieutenant Henry O'Brien was more severely wounded at the Battle of Deep Bottom, which ended his Civil War service. Nineteen years later he had surgery on his right shoulder, which removed 22 pieces of bone and bullet fragments. He died in St. Louis in 1902.

Other Maine men in the 1st Minnesota who were killed or wounded at Gettysburg include: William Bassett of Lowell (W), Philander Ellis of Mayfield (K), Henry Fifield of Corinna (K), Jonathon Goodrich of Bingham (W), William Harmon of Lee (W), Alonso Hayden of Somerset (K), Thomas Nason of Crawford (W), and Benjamin Staples of Cornish (W).

*William Lockran, "The First Minnesota at Gettysburg" in *Glimpses of the Nation's Struggle,* Volume 3 (St. Paul: 1893), page 37-38. Lochran was the regiment historian.

The Long March

Route marching by army corps during the Civil War followed a given set of rules. The order of march had to be determined by division, brigade, regiment, and company, along with the position in line of supply wagons and artillery. The men would march using a "common step" of about 28-30 inches, covering 210 feet, or 90 paces, per minute. At this pace, the corps could cover a mile in about 25 minutes or two miles an hour with the prescribed 10-minute rest every hour. The shorter men in the company would march in front, keeping the taller men in the back from lengthening the pace. At this rate the army could cover 15-20 miles in a day. On longer marches, the accordion effect of stopping and starting was lessened, allowing the march to proceed smoothly (anyone who has been in a traffic jam on a freeway understands the accordion effect).

There were some legendary long marches during the Civil War. Confederate General A. P. Hill's division covered the 17-mile march from Harper's Ferry to Sharpsburg, Maryland, in 8 hours on September 17, 1862, arriving just in time to save the day at the Battle of Antietam. Stonewall Jackson's brigade covered 40 miles in one two-day period in March of 1862 during the Valley Campaign through difficult mountainous terrain. During that same campaign, Union General Nathaniel Banks's army retreated 35 miles (in bad order) in 14 hours following the First Battle of Winchester in May of 1862. General William T. Sherman's "March to the Sea" in 1864 covered almost 300 miles, but it was done leisurely over a six week period.

None of these match the record of the Union 6th Corps (including the 5th, 6th, and 7th Maine Regiments) on the evening of July 1, 1863 and the following day. Marching from their camp site in Manchester, Maryland, the 13,500 member corps covered 38 miles in 17 hours (the mileage is actually in dispute — during the first part of the march, orders were received to change routes, causing several miles of back tracking — the actual total for the march might be up to 42 miles). Starting at 9:00 p.m., the first eight hours of the march were done in the dead of night. This was following by nine hours of marching in the heat of the summer sun. Men dropped out of line by the score, suffering from heat stroke and exhaustion. Little time was given for food breaks, rest times were shortened or skipped completely. After a grueling march, advance elements of the 6th Corps reached the Gettysburg battlefield by 2:00 p.m. on July 2, while most of its regiments arrived between 4:00 and 5:00 p.m., serving as the reserve of the army. They had completed "The Long March."

HELD IN RESERVE
5th, 6th, and 7th Maine Regiments

Colonel Clark S. Edwards

The 5th, 6th, and 7th Maine Regiments were all mustered into service between June and August of 1861. The 5th Maine, originally under the command of Colonel Mark H. Dunnell of Portland, was made up of men from central and southern Maine. Three of its ten companies were from Portland, so the regiment became known as the "Forrest City Regiment." During the Civil War, the 5th Maine captured more battle flags than any other Maine regiment, participating in twenty-two battles from First Bull Run to Petersburg. At the battle of Gettysburg, Clark S. Edwards, a farmer from Bethel, served as colonel of the regiment.[92]

The 6th Maine Regiment was originally commanded by Colonel Abner Knowles of Bangor with Lieutenant Colonel Hiram Burnham of Cherryfield as second in command.

Formed from the coastal areas of Eastern Maine, the 6th Maine was most famous for its successful charge up Marye's Heights at Fredericksburg on May 3, 1863, a position that was thought to be impregnable. Charging with bayonets, with uncapped guns to prevent the men from stopping to fire, the regiment lost 128 of the less than 400 men who began the charge. Color Sergeant John Gray of Eastport, a barrel maker by trade, "the bravest or the craziest man in the regiment," was the first man over the top as he planted the flag.[93]

The 7th Maine Regiment, originally commanded by Colonel Edwin C. Mason of Portland, with Lieutenant Colonel Seldon Conner of Fairfield as second in command, included two companies each raised from Aroostook, Kennebec, and Penobscot counties.[94] During its service

Lieutenant Colonel Hiram Burnham

Lieutenant Colonel Seldon Connor

from the Peninsula Campaign in 1862 to the Valley Campaign of 1864, the regiment suffered 52 killed in action or died of their wounds (with another 212 men dying from various diseases); 403 men wounded in action and nineteen men perishing in Confederate prisoner-of-war camps. The regiment is most famous for its actions during the Battle of Antietam, where, under the command of Major Thomas W. Hyde of Bath, the regiment advanced to the Piper Farm, the farthest advance of any regiment on that portion of the field. The regiment also participated in the charge up Marye's Heights at Fredericksburg in May of 1863.

As part of General Sedgwick's 6th Corps, these three regiments participated in the "Long March" to Gettysburg, arriving in the early evening of July 2. Here they were sent to various spots on the battlefield to act as reserve forces. The 5th Maine took a position near the northern base of Little Round Top, the 6th Maine found itself to the east and rear of the Round Tops along the Taneytown Road, and the 7th Maine was moved from position to position during the night of July 2, getting very little rest, eventually taking a position along Rock Creek near the Baltimore Pike and taking part in only some sporadic skirmish fire. Two men in the regiment were killed during the battle, including Private Richard Scully of Castleton, New Brunswick.

We Stand on Guard for Thee — Canadians in the American Civil War

Canada did not become a federated nation until 1867, two years after the end of the Civil War. During the war, it was a group of English colonies (Newfoundland, Nova Scotia, New Brunswick, and Prince Edward Island), the United Province of Canada (parts of present day Quebec and Ontario), and Rupert's Land (the area of the Hudson Bay drainage area). Canada's unification happened partially because of tensions between England and the United States during the American Civil War, invasion concerns, and the Fenian Raids (Irish Civil War veterans attempting to conquer Canada, including an interesting attempt to capture Campobello Island in 1866). Approximately 15,000 draft dodgers fled to Canada during the war, many fleeing across the Maine border.

In contrast, between 33,000 to 55,000 men from Canada crossed the border to fight in the Civil War, all except a few hundred fighting for the Union cause (nearly 3,000 of them served in Maine units or enlisted in the navy in Maine). A few became famous during and after the war. Calixa Levalee joined the Union army and became a lieutenant in the 4th Rhode Island Regiment. A trained musician, after the war he wrote the music to accompany a patriotic poem called "O Canada," which eventually became the national anthem of the country in 1980. Canadian born Edward P. Doherty, as a lieutenant in the 16th New York Cavalry, led the detachment that captured John Wilkes Booth in April of 1865.

Thirty-two Canadians are listed on the rolls of Maine regiments at Gettysburg:

REGIMENT	NAME	TOWN/PROVINCE
1st Maine Cavalry	William R. Snow	Woodstock, New Brunswick
3rd Maine Regiment	Archibald Campbell	Cape Breton, Nova Scotia
6th Maine Battery	Thomas Bonnar	Frederickton, New Brunswick
	Timothy Hegarty	Miramichi, New Brunswick
5th Maine Regiment	Patrick Brady	St. John, New Brunswick
	Joseph Paradis	Quebec, C.E.
	Clark Whaland	St. John, New Brunswick
6th Maine Regiment	Michael Condon	St. Stephen, New Brunswick
	John Connell	Halifax, Nova Scotia
	Frederick Dans	Moncton, New Brunswick
	Allen Green	Blissville, New Brunswick
	Robinson Kitching	Frederickton, New Brunswick
	Peter McDonald	Pictou, Nova Scotia

	Thomas Mackey	Halifax, Nova Scotia
	Henri Myer	Moncton, New Brunswick
	Elias Smith	St. Stephen, New Brunswick
	William H. Tower	Sackville, Nova Scotia
7th Maine Regiment	John E. Bailey	Frederickton, New Brunswick
	Robert Clark	St. John, New Brunswick
	William H. Duprach	Halifax, Nova Scotia
	Charles Pembroke	Gageboro, Nova Scotia
	Richard Scully	Castleton, New Brunswick
	James Sullivan	St. John, New Brunswick
10th Maine Battalion	John Beardsley	Grand Falls, New Brunswick
	Edward Gillis	Miramichi, New Brunswick
	Edward Lee	Magaguadavic, New Brunswick
	Archibald McDougal	Prince Edward Island
16th Maine Regiment	John Downey	Windsor, Nova Scotia
17th Maine Regiment	Peter McDonald	Compton, Canada
20th Maine Regiment	Glazier Estabrook	Burton, New Brunswick
	George W. Leach	Unknown, New Brunswick
	Alexander E. Lester	St. John, New Brunswick

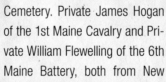

Richard Scully, of the 7th Maine, was killed in a skirmish at Gettysburg very near to where the 7th Maine monument is located. He is buried in the Maine section of the Gettysburg National Cemetery. Private James Hogan of the 1st Maine Cavalry and Private William Flewelling of the 6th Maine Battery, both from New Brunswick, are not listed on the rolls, but are listed as deserters, Hogan on July 6, 1863 and Flewelling on July 9, 1863.

Joseph Paradis enlisted as a private in the 5th Maine Regiment and rose to the rank of 2nd Lieutenant. At the battle of Rappahannock Station, he captured thirteen Confederate soldiers and a stand of colors. He died of wounds suffered at the Battle of Cold Harbor (1864). Members of the 5th Maine took up a collection to have his body embalmed and sent back to his family in Quebec.

10th Maine Battalion

The 10th Maine Regiment was a reorganization of the 1st Maine Regiment, a unit that had signed up at the beginning of the Civil War as a three month regiment. The 10th Maine mustered in on October 5, 1861 to serve the remainder of two years of service to end in May of 1863. Made up of men mostly from western Maine (with the exception of Company D, which was originally men from Aroostook County), the regiment served with distinction in the eastern theater of the war until the end of their enlistment period.[95]

However, 244 men in the regiment had signed three-year enlistment papers, so a three company battalion was formed and detailed as the provost guard of the 12th Corps under the command of Captain John D. Beardsley of Grand Falls, New Brunswick.

At Gettysburg, 205 men in the battalion were present and performed a number of duties, including guarding a cattle herd and marching Confederate prisoners to the rear. Around noon on July 2nd, General Henry Slocum, commander of the 12th Corps, asked for six men from the battalion to go on a scouting expedition, without weapons, to find out if any Confederate forces were lurking to the east and rear of the Federal army. If captured they were to pretend that they were looking for water. Sergeant James Tarr of Biddeford, Sergeant Henry Kallock of Ashland, Sergeant Charles Anderson of Smyrna, Private Henry Cole of Woodstock, Private Sydney Fletcher of Biddeford, and one other unnamed soldier then went on a two-hour adventure.

Sergeant's Kallock and Anderson, both from Aroostook County and thus experienced woodsmen, went off by themselves, eventually just missing capture and avoiding fire from rebel skirmishers. Tarr, Cole, Fletcher, and the unknown member of the group actually moved at least a mile before coming to an opening near a house. There Sergeant Tarr saw some Confederate soldiers watching the group. Pretending not to see them, he casually explained to the others that they would have to run at his signal, which they did. The rebels fired at them but missed. All six men made it back to report to General Slocum. It is not sure they accomplished much, except to have a story to tell their grandchildren.

THE VISION PLACE OF SOULS
The Dedication of Maine Monuments at Gettysburg — *October 2-3, 1889*

The Gettysburg Springs Hotel, which opened in 1869, became a popular stop for veterans and sightseers interested in touring the Gettysburg battlefield. A horse trolley rail line brought visitors from the town to the hotel. Located just to the east of Herr's Ridge (the site of some of the first day's fighting), the hotel was very close to Katalysine Springs (originally Lithia Springs), a water source that was not part of nearby Willoughby Run. The springs were reputed to have curative powers, although this fact was not discovered until after the battle when the tourists started showing up. Katalysine Springs Water was immediately endorsed by Andrew Curtin, Pennsylvania Governor during the Civil War, General George Meade, and other luminaries of the conflict for its therapeutic value.[96]

On Wednesday evening, October 2, 1889, the members of the 20th Maine Regimental Association held their annual reunion at the Gettysburg Springs Hotel. In attendance were thirty-one veterans, several wives, and one son, attendees included Joshua Chamberlain, Holman Melcher, Theodore Gerrish, and honorary member John B. Bachelder, who had served in the position as Superintendent of Tablets and Legends for the Gettysburg Battlefield Memorial Association. The Regimental Association usually met at various places in Maine, but this year was special. On the following day, the Maine monuments erected on the battlefield were to be dedicated.

Following supper, the meeting was called to order by President Melcher. The reports of the secretary and treasurer were read and approved. Chamberlain, Bachelder, and Captain Howard Prince of Cumberland gave brief remarks about the following day's activities. The question of allowing sons of members to become members was tabled and a committee was formed to prepare resolutions of sympathy to Mrs. General Gouverneur Warren. This was followed by a reading of a poem, "The Maltese Cross," by Samuel L. Miller of Waldoboro, and a final benediction by Theodore Gerrish.

Charles Hamlin — Keeper of the Record

Charles Hamlin knew how to collect and save records. Trained as a lawyer, Hamlin during a long career served as Assistant Adjutant General in the Union Army, City Solicitor of the City of Bangor, U.S. Register in Bankruptcy, and as reporter of decisions of the Maine Supreme Court. This experience in record keeping came in handy when he became Chairman of the Executive Committee of the Maine Gettysburg Commission. In 1898, the commission published *Maine at Gettysburg*, a 602-page account that is still the essential reference work for those who wish to study the actions of Maine troops at that battle. Hamlin wrote the introduction to that volume and was instrumental in its publication. He was also a leader in the Gettysburg Battlefield Memorial Association.

The second son of Vice President Hannibal Hamlin, Charles Hamlin graduated from Bowdoin College in 1857 at the age of twenty. During the Civil War he served on the staff of the 2nd Division of the Union 3rd Corps and was present at the Battle of Gettysburg. Brevetted a Brigadier General at the end of the war, he and his sister Sarah were at Ford's Theater the night President Lincoln was assassinated. Following the war, Hamlin became a leading expert in bankruptcy law, authoring a book on the subject. He served as President of the Eastern Maine General Hospital (now Eastern Maine Medical Center) in Bangor and as a trustee of the Penobscot Savings Bank. Elected to the Maine Legislature in 1883, he served as Speaker of the Maine House of Representatives during his second term. A record keeper to the end of his life in 1911, his papers make up a major portion of the Hamlin Family Collection at the Raymond H. Fogler Library at the University of Maine in Orono.

On the next day, festivities began with the firing of a national salute on Cemetery Hill at 9:00 a.m. Then the delegation, led by Maine Governor Edwin Chick Burleigh of Linneus and Hannibal Hamlin, former vice president during the war, and other dignitaries, began a tour of the Maine monuments on the battlefield. At each stop speeches were made, "Taps" was played, stories were told, and tears were shed as middle-aged comrades held regimental reunions. That evening, at 8:00 p.m., at the Adams County Courthouse on Baltimore and West Middle Streets (the courthouse had served as both a command post and as a hospital, for both Union and Confederate armies during the battle), the official dedication program took place.

Addresses were made by Chamberlain, as President of the Day, and Charles Hamlin, as Chairman of the Maine Gettysburg Commission. An oration of some length was given by Seldon Connor, ex-governor of Maine and Lt. Colonel of the 7th Maine Regiment, and was well received. A presentation of the monuments was made by Governor Burleigh, followed by a response to accept from Governor James A. Beaver of Pennsylvania. Then, finally, a benediction was spoken by the Reverand G. R. Palmer, a member of the 19th Maine Regiment.

At the end of his powerful oration, Chamberlain spoke words that ring true to this day:

> But these monuments are not to commemorate the dead alone. Death was but the divine acceptance of life freely offered by everyone. Service was the central fact. That fact and that truth these monuments commemorate. They mark the centres around which stood the manhood of Maine, steadfast in noble service — to the uttermost, to the uppermost! Those who fell here those who have fallen before or since those who linger, yet a little longer soon to follow; all are mustered in one great company on the shining heights of life, with that star of Maine's armorial ensign upon their foreheads forever — like the ranks of the galaxy.
>
> In great deeds something abides. On great fields something stays. Forms change and pass; bodies disappear; but spirits linger to consecrate ground for the vision place of souls. And reverent men and women from afar, and generations that know us not, and that we know not of, heart drawn to see where and by whom great things were suffered and done for them, shall come to this deathless field, to ponder and dream; and lo! the shadow of a mighty presence shall wrap them in its bosom, and the power of the vision pass into their souls.[97]

NOTES

85. For a long time, the focus on the Battle of Gettysburg was all about the legend of Pickett's Charge. In reality, the battle had been decided on the second day. All General Lee did on July 3 was turn a draw into a loss.

86. *Maine at Gettysburg*, page 296.

87. On July 3, the 19th Maine lost an additional 75 men during the cannonade

and Pickett's charge, bringing the two day total to 215 casualties, the second largest number of casualties in the battle of any Maine regiment behind the 16th Maine, amounting to a casualty rate of 53% (however, most of the 16th Maine casualties were captured as prisoners while most of the 19th Maine casualties were killed or wounded).

88. The 3,226 number includes men from the 1st District of Columbia Cavalry, who were transferred into the 1st Maine Cavalry, subtracting them gives a total of 2,895 men from Maine who served in the regiment.

89. *Maine at Gettysburg*, page 493.

90. Ibid., page 495.

91. Tobie, Edward P., *History of the First Maine Cavalry* (Boston: 1887), page 177.

92. Following the war, Edwards gave the dedication address for the regiment's monument at Gettysburg in 1889. He later supervised the construction of the Maine building at the Columbian Exposition in Chicago in 1893 which can now be seen in Poland Spring, Maine.

93. Mundy, James H., *No Rich Men's Sons, the Sixth Maine Volunteer Infantry* (Cape Elizabeth, 1994), page 116. Sergeant Gray would repeat this feat at the Battle of Rappahannock Station in November of 1863 but it would cost him his life.

94. Colonel Mason did not take command until November of 1861 as his commission to serve in the volunteer service was not approved until then.

95. The 10th Maine was quite famous for its drum corps, often thought to be the largest and best drilled in the Army of the Potomac.

96. The hotel burned to the ground in 1917. The land was eventually taken over by the Gettysburg County Club golf course until it was purchased by the National Park Service in 2011.

97. *Maine at Gettysburg*, pages 558-559.

THE ORDER OF BATTLE – MAINE REGIMENTS AT GETTYSBURG

Major General George G. Meade – Commanding
Major General Daniel Butterfield – Chief of Staff
Brigadier General Seth Williams – Assistant Adjutant General (Maine)
Brigadier General Henry J. Hunt – Chief of Artillery
Brigadier General Gouverneur Warren – Chief of Engineers
Brigadier General Rufus Ingalls – Chief Quartermaster (Maine)
Brigadier General Marsena R. Patrick – Provost Marshall

(C) Captured (K) Killed (MW) Mortally Wounded (W) Wounded

Corps Headquarters	Division	Brigade	Regiment
First Corps Maj. Gen. John F. Reynolds (K) Maj. Gen. Abner Doubleday Maj. Gen. John Newton **1st ME Cavalry/Co. L** Capt. Constantine Taylor	**Second Division** Brig. Gen. John C. Robinson	**First Brigade** Brig. Gen. Gabriel R. Paul (W) Col. Samuel H. Leonard (W) Col. Adrian R. Root (W/C) Col. Richard Coulter (W) Col. Peter Lyle	**16th Maine** Col. Charles W. Tilden (C) Lt. Col. Augustus B. Farnum
		Artillery Brigade Col. Charles S. Wainwright	**Hall's 2nd ME Battery** Capt. James A. Hall **Steven's 5th ME Battery** Capt. Greenlief T. Stevens (W) Lt. Edward N. Whittier
Second Corps Maj. Gen. Winfield S. Hancock (W) Brig. Gen. John Gibbon (W) Brig. Gen. William Hays	**First Division** Brig. Gen. John C. Caldwell (Maine)		
	Second Division Brig. Gen. John Gibbon (W) Brig. Gen. William Harrow	**First Brigade** Brig. Gen. William Harrow Col. Frances E. Heath	**19th Maine** Col. Francis E. Heath Lt. Col. Henry W. Cunningham

Corps Headquarters	Division	Brigade	Regiment
Third Corps Maj. Gen. Daniel E. Sickles (W) Mag. Gen. David B. Birney	**First Division** Maj. Gen. David B. Birney Brig. Gen. J. H. Hobart Ward	**Second Brigade** Brig. Gen. J. H. Hobart Ward Col. Hiram Berdan	**3rd Maine** Col. Moses B. Lakeman Maj. Samuel P. Lee **4th Maine** Col. Elijah Walker (W) Maj. Ebenezer Whitcomb (MW) Capt. Edwin Libby **2nd U.S Sharp-shooters** Maj. Homer R. Stoughton Capt. Jacob McClure
		Third Brigade Col. P. Regis de Trobriand	**17th Maine** Lt. Col. Charles B. Merrill Maj. George W. West
	Second Division Brig. Gen. Andrew A. Humphreys Maj. Chales Hamlin Assistant Adjutant General (Maine)		
Fifth Corps Maj. Gen. George Sykes	**First Division** Brig. Gen. George Barnes (W)	**Third Brigade** Col. Vincent Strong (MW) Col. James. C. Rice	**20th Maine** Col. Joshua L. Chamberlain
Sixth Corps Maj. Gen. John Sedgwick	**First Division** Brig. Gen. Horatio G. Wright	**Second Brigade** Brig. Gen. Joseph A. Bartlett Col. Emery Upton	**5th Maine** Col. Clark S. Edwards
		Third Brigade Brig. Gen. David A. Russell	**6th Maine** Col. Hiram Burnham
	Second Division Brig. Gen. Albion P. Howe (Maine)	**Third Brigade** Brig. Gen. Thomas H. Neill	**7th Maine** Lt. Col. Seldon Connor

Corps Headquarters	Division	Brigade	Regiment
Eleventh Corps Maj. Gen. Oliver Otis Howard (Maine) Maj. Gen. Carl Shurtz	**First Division** Brig. Gen. Francis C. Barlow (W) Brig. Gen. Adelbert Ames (Maine)	**Second Brigade** Brig. Gen. Adelbert Ames (Maine)	
Twelfth Corps Maj. Gen. Henry W. Slocum **10th Maine Battalion/ Provost Guard** Col. George Lafayette Beal			
Cavalry Corps Maj. Gen. Alfred Pleasonton	**Second Division** Brig. Gen. David Gregg	**Third Brigade** Col. John I. Gregg	**1st Maine Cavalry** Lt. Col. Charles H. Smith
Artillery Reserve Brig. Gen. Robert O. Tyler		**First Volunteer Brigade** Lt. Col. Freeman McGilvery (Maine) **Fourth Volunteer Brigade** Capt. Robert H. Fitzhugh	**Dow's 6th Maine Battery** Lt. Edwin B. Dow

APPENDIX
A Driving Tour of

MAINE MONUMENTS AT GETTYSBURG

Gettysburg National Military Park is located in Adams County, Pennsylvania. By car — the National Park Service Museum and Visitor Center is located at 1195 Baltimore Pike (Rte. 97) with a back entrance from the Taneytown Road (State Rt. 134). From north or south, follow US 15 to Gettysburg and watch for signs to direct you to the visitor center. The signs are near the exit at Rte. 97. Go north on Rte. 97 and look for the entrance, which will be on your left at the stoplight. From East or West, drive into Gettysburg on US Rte. 30, turn South on Baltimore Street (Rte. 97), and follow signs to the entrance, which will be on your right at the stoplight.

By air — Harrisburg International Airport at Middletown, Pennsylvania, approximately 35 miles north of Gettysburg is the closest air terminal. The second closest is Baltimore-Washington International near Baltimore, Maryland. Taking Interstate 70 west from there and then Highway 15 north to Gettysburg is a ninety mile trip. Maryland Rte. 140 is more direct at about 60 miles. Philadelphia is 140 miles away.

The park is open daily from 6:00 a.m. to 10:00 p.m. April 1 to October 31, and 6:00 a.m. to 7:00 p.m. November 1 to March 31. Park hours are strictly enforced. The Museum and Visitor Center is open daily throughout the year. The center is closed on Thanksgiving Day, Christmas Day, and New Years Day. The Museum and Visitor Center hours of operation are 8:00 a.m. to 5:00 p.m. October 1 through March 31, and 8:00 a.m. to 6:00 p.m. April 1 to September 30.

THE TOUR

From the center circle in the town of Gettysburg go west by car on Chambersburg Street to Chambersburg Pike (Rte. 30) then drive to the following stops.

Hall's 2nd Maine Artillery Monument, Chambersburg Pike — *July 1, 1863*
Map coordinates - 39.837848° N , 77.251547° W.

The 2nd Maine Battery was commanded at the Battle of Gettysburg by Captain James A. Hall. It was part of the 1st Corps Artillery Brigade, and brought 127 men to the field serving six Ordnance Rifles, suffering 18 wounded. The monument is near the Stone Avenue intersection and the Major General John Reynolds statute. Notice that General Reynolds's horse has two feet off the ground, following the unofficial rule (or coincidence) to indicate that its rider was killed in the battle (one foot off the ground means the rider was wounded in the battle).

Looking to the west down the Chambersburg Pike, you can imagine General Henry Heth's Division of Hill's Corps moving east toward your position. To the north, in the distance, you can see the 1938 Peace Memorial on Oak Hill.

Walking 75 yards north, you will come to the infamous railroad cut that the 42nd Mississippi Regiment used to flank Hall's Battery, forcing it to retreat to the east.

Getting back in your car, take the first left off the Chambersburg Pike onto Stone/ Meredith Avenue, you will soon see several monuments on your left and right, including one dedicated to Farmer John Burns, a 69-year-old private citizen of Gettysburg, who joined the Iron Brigade to fight the Confederates. Continue on until you come to the intersection of Reynolds Avenue — a brief stop will put you opposite a statue of Major General Abner Doubleday, who took over command of the 1st Corps at the death of General Reynolds.

Turn left onto Reynolds Avenue and cross over the Chambersburg Pike at the light. This will take you over a bridge crossing the railroad cut. Continue on until taking a right on Buford Avenue then a left turn onto Doubleday Avenue. This will take you to:

16th Maine Monument, Doubleday Avenue — *July 1, 1863*
Map Coordinates - 39.841588° N, 77.242832° W.

The 16th Maine Infantry was commanded at the Battle of Gettysburg by Colonel Charles W. Tilden. The regiment fought for much of the afternoon of July 1 at the location of its main monument. When the Union position collapsed, the regiment was moved to the point along Mummasburg Road and ordered to serve as the rear guard to buy time for Doubleday's Division to withdraw from Oak Ridge. Much of the regiment was captured, wounded or killed.

Walk or drive up to the intersection of Doubleday Avenue and the Mummasburg Road. There on the right you will find the marker showing the location of the 16th Maine Regiment as it made its final stand. There is an observation tower nearby that gives a good view to the north and east of the struggle between Confederate General Ewell's 2nd Corps and the 11th Corps of the Union Army.

Here you have the choice to continue across the Mummasburg Road to visit the 1938 Peace Memorial or retrace your Rte. back to the Chambersburg Pike.

Turning left onto the Chambersburg Pike, drive east to make the first right onto Seminary Avenue. There on the right you will come to:

Stevens's 5th Maine Battery Marker, Seminary Ridge — *July 1, 1863*
Map Coordinates - 39.833741° N, 77.244946° W. 1863

The 5th Maine Battery was commanded at the Battle of Gettysburg by Captain Greenlief Thurlow Stevens. He was wounded on July 2, and Lieutenant Edward N. Whittier took command. Whittier went on to be awarded the Medal of Honor for his actions at Fisher's Hill in 1864. The 5th Maine Battery brought 136 men to the field serving six twelve-pounder Napoleons. It suffered 3 killed, 13 wounded, and 7 missing during the battle.

At this point, the battery was firing on positions to the west. On the left of the avenue is the famous Lutheran Theological Seminary, the oldest continuing Lutheran seminary in North America. The cupola of the Old Dorm, made famous in the movie *Gettysburg*, was an observation post for both sides during the battle. After the battle the

seminary became a hospital until September of 1863. The cupola was hit by lightning in 1913, but it was restored in the 1950s.

Continue south on Seminary Avenue, crossing the Fairfield Road (Rte. 116) at the light onto West Confederate Avenue. Soon to the left you will see the very impressive

Virginia Monument topped by a statue of Robert E. Lee, sculpted by F. William Sievers and dedicated in 1917. Lee stares across the Pickett's Charge field at the Union lines three quarters of a mile away.

As you continue on West Confederate Avenue, you will turn right onto Berdan Avenue and drive to a small circle, coming to:

3rd Maine Regiment Marker, Berdan Avenue — *July 2, 1863*
Map Coordinates - 39.808004° N, 77.257255° W.

The 3rd Maine was commanded at the Battle of Gettysburg by Colonel Moses B. Lakeman. Lakeman took over the brigade on July 3, and Captain William C. Morgan took command of the regiment. The regiment was sent forward from its position near the Emmitsburg Road along with the 1st U.S. Sharpshooters regiment to determine if Confederate forces were flanking the Union Army. Here the regiment fought a brief but sharp engagement with troops from Alabama before retreating back to its original position. This position represents the furthest advance by Union troops on the second day of the battle. The importance of this action cannot be overstated. It confirmed General Sickles's belief that the Confederate army was attempting a flanking movement. It led to his decision to advance the entire 3rd Corps to the Emmitsburg Road, a decision that has caused much controversy since.

A short walk to the west through the woods (there are paths) will bring you to open fields where the actual Confederate flanking movement took place. At this point, to the south, you can see the Eisenhower National Historic Site.

Returning to your car, leave Berdan Avenue, turn right back onto West Confederate Avenue, and continue on this road. Soon, to the right, you can catch a glimpse through the trees of the newest Confederate statue, that of General James Longstreet. After crossing the Millerstown Road, you will come to the Warfield Ridge Observation Tower, which is worth the climb.

Crossing the Emmitsburg Road onto South Confederate Avenue you will soon come to a dirt road to your left. Take that road, and the first left, then walk right down the Slyder Farm Lane to:

2nd U.S. Sharpshooters, Company D Marker, Slyder Farm — *July 2, 1863*
Map Coordinates - 39.790598 N, 77.249618W.

Company D of the 2nd U.S. Sharp-shooters had 27 men from Maine. As the best riflemen in the army, these men were sent forward to this spot as skirmishers to protect the left flank of the 3rd Corps. Looking to the south from this spot you can see the monuments of Hood's Division of Long-street's Corps on Warfield Ridge along South Confederate Avenue. As these troops began their attack, the Sharpshooters fell back toward Devil's Den, some joining with the 4th Maine Regiment in its fight there.

Drive back up the dirt road to South Confederate Avenue. Turn left and continue, along the way you will see the Texas, Alabama, and Soldiers and Sailors Monuments, ahead of you is the summit of Big Round Top. Continue until you see a small parking area as you go up the drive to the left, this is:

20th Maine Marker, Big Round Top — *July 2, 1863*
Map Coordinates - 39.786642°N, 77.239544° W.

Take the path across the road from the parking lot to the summit of Big Round Top. Take your time, it is a steep hill. There you will find the 20th Maine marker. The regiment occupied this position during the night of July 2, 1863 until moved to reserve behind Cemetery Ridge on the morning of July 3, 1863.

Return down the hill to your car and continue on South Confederate Avenue. Take the next right onto Wright Avenue, you will immediately see a small three-car parking lot that the Park Service, in its wisdom, put there soon after the Ken Burns *Civil War* series in 1990, when Joshua Chamberlain became a folk hero. Park there for:

20th Maine Monument, Little Round Top — *July 2, 1863*
Map Coordinates - 39.789476° N, 77.236146° W.

It was at this spot that the 385 men of the 20th Maine Regiment, led by Colonel Joshua L. Chamberlain, stopped the flanking movement of the 15th Alabama Regiment. As you look down across the parking lot, you can see where the Alabama troops attacked as they came down from Big Round Top. To the right, the 20th Maine line extends along a short stone wall.

Walking down the path to the parking lot, turn left to find a narrow dirt lane. Follow this path about 100 yards to a small marker showing the position of the 20th Maine's Company B. Sent to the left, to guard the flank and soon joined by some sharpshooters, the company charged, attacking the right flank of the enemy at the same time that the rest of the regiment charged down the hill, capturing several hundred members of the 15th Alabama.

Returning to your car, continue east along Wright Avenue crossing the Taneytown Road. There you will come to:

6th Maine Monument, Wright Avenue — *July 2-3, 1863*
Map Coordinates - 39.783435° N, 77.228407° W.

The 6th Maine was commanded at the Battle of Gettysburg by Colonel Hiram Burnham. It brought 439 men to the field and suffered no casualties, being held in reserve with Howe's brigade of the 6th Corps in the rear of Big Round Top along Taneytown Road.

Retrace your steps to the intersection of Wright Avenue and South Confederate Avenue, turn right as it becomes Sykes Avenue. Drive to the top of the hill and park for:

Little Round Top — *July 2, 1863*
Map Coordinates - 39.792516° N, 77.236683° W.

Although there are no Maine markers or monuments on the summit of Little Round Top, you do not want to miss the opportunity to see the view looking down on the "Valley of Death." Be sure to rub Patrick O'Rourke's nose for good luck, then climb to the top of the 44th New York monument for the best view down to Devil's Den and the 4th Maine monument to the right of the photograph. Also be sure to visit the statue of General Warren and look for the monument to Colonel Strong Vincent, considered by many to be the real hero of Little Round Top. The Vincent monument is on the slope southward and down from the 44th New York monument at the spot where he was mortally wounded.

Returning to your car, continue down Sykes Avenue, taking the next left down the Wheatfield Road, then turning left onto Crawford Avenue. Little Round Top is to your left. Continue to take the right onto Warren Avenue, there you will find a parking lot to the left. Park there for:

4th Maine Monument, Devil's Den — *July 2, 1863*
Map Coordinates - 39.791882° N, 77.241421° W

The 4th Maine was commanded at Gettysburg by Colonel Elijah Walker, who designed the Devil's Den monument. Colonel Walker was wounded on July 2, and Captain Edwin Libby took command. The regiment brought 332 men to the field as it held back the elements of Arkansas, Alabama, and Georgia regiments until overwhelmed, retreating back to the safety of Cemetery Ridge. To the east, Little Round Top dominates the battlefield, to the west are the unusually large boulders of Devil's Den.

Back in the car, follow the avenue around Devil's Den and through some woods until you get to an open area and the intersection with DeTrobriand Avenue. There are parking spaces to the right, stop there for:

17th Maine Monument, the Wheatfield — *July 2, 1863*
Map Coordinates - 39.795746° N, 77.244412° W.

This monument, dedicated in 1888, is by far the most elaborate Maine monument on the battlefield. Behind the monument, along the line of trees of Rose Woods, is the short stone wall that the 17th Maine held against repeated attacks from Confederate General Anderson's brigade of Georgians. To the east is the Wheatfield, looking very much like it did in 1863. Very close to the monument, down DeTrobriand Avenue, is the monument of the 115th Pennsylvania. When this monument was dedicated a year later in 1889, it caused a flurry of complaints from members of the 17th Maine, claiming that the Pennsylvanians were nowhere near the fight.

Continue on what is now Sickles Avenue, driving around the loop. Along this part of the battlefield are several interesting monuments. My favorite is the Irish Brigade monument with Celtic Cross and Wolfhound.

Turn left onto the Wheatfield Road, traveling west until taking a left turn into the Peach Orchard. Park on the road for:

3rd Maine Monument, the Peach Orchard — *July 2, 1863*
Map Coordinates — 39.800411° N, 77.250067° W.

This is by far the most unusual Maine monument on the battlefield, with a large cube of Maine granite on the top. The 3rd Maine was commanded at the Battle of Gettysburg by Colonel Moses B. Lakeman. Lakeman took over the brigade on July 3, and Captain William C. Morgan took command of the regiment. The 3rd Maine held here until overwhelmed by Confederate General Kershaw's brigade of South Carolinians and General Barksdale's Mississippians.

Backtrack east down the Wheatfield Road, past the Valley of Death to take a left onto Sedgwick Avenue. Park immediately on the right to find:

5th Maine Monument, Sedgwick Avenue — *Evening of July 2- July 3, 1863*

Map Coordinates — 39.795311° N, 77.235006° W.

The inscription on this monument reads "5th Maine Infantry 2nd Brig. 1st Div. 6th Corps. Occupied this position from evening of July 2nd until close of battle. Mustered into the U.S. Service Portland, Me. June 24, 1861. Served with the Army of the Potomac in the field from Bull Run to Petersburg. Mustered out, Portland, June 27, 1864."

The 6th Corps was held in reserve during the Battle of Gettysburg, so these men participated in no fighting and suffered no casualties.

Returning to your car, continue on Sedgwick Avenue, it eventually becomes South Hancock Avenue, soon you will park on the right to find:

Dow's 6th Maine Battery, South Hancock Avenue — *July 3, 1863*

Map Coordinates — 39.803292° N, 77.234534° W.

This monument stands over eleven feet high and is carved from granite, with the pyramid of cannon balls at its top carved from black Addison granite. A relief of the star symbol of the 5th Corps is on the front of the monument, and below it a relief of flags, a drum, a cannon barrel, artillery ramrod, and a sword. The monument was dedicated on October 3, 1889 by the State of Maine.

Lieutenant Edwin B. Dow commanded this battery of 103 men, serving four 12-pounder Napoleons. The battery suffered thirteen men wounded in the artillery duel that preceded Pickett's Charge on the afternoon of July 3.

Across the road and a few paces up is a statue of Father William Corby standing on the very boulder that he stood on to bless the troops before the battle on July 2, 1863. Eventually he became the President of Notre Dame University. An exact replica of this statue is located on the campus near Corby Hall, where people say he is signaling for a football "fair catch."

Continue north on South Hancock Avenue, before coming to the large Pennsylvania Monument, park to find to the left:

1st Minnesota Monument — *July 2, 1863*
Map Coordinates — 39.8066000N, 77.2350170W.

The 1st Minnesota at this spot was sent into battle on July 2, 1863 by General Hancock in a desperate attempt to buy time while waiting for reinforcements to stop the last charge of Wilcox's brigade. Sending 262 men into the breach, only 47 men returned after the fight. To the left of this position the 19th Maine Regiment forced Lang's Florida Brigade to retreat while suffering almost 200 casualties.

On the following day, the flag bearer of the 1st Minnesota, Henry O'Brien, picked up the fallen flag of the regiment during Pickett's Charge and carried a wounded comrade to safety. For this he was awarded the Medal of Honor. O'Brien was born in Calais, Maine, in 1842.

Past the Pennsylvania monument the road becomes North Hancock Avenue. Drive to parking spaces on the right side of the road next to a small grouping of trees. Here you will find:

19th Maine Monument — *July 3, 1863, Pickett's Charge*

Map Coordinates — 39.81106° N, 77.23612° W.

There is a lot to see at this stop. The High Water of the Confederacy tablet is near the copse of trees, to the right is Cushing's Battery and the spot where Confederate General Lewis Armistead was mortally wounded. Going down the line to the left you will find the 19th Maine monument, perhaps the heaviest Maine monument on the battlefield. The 19th Maine was commanded at the Battle of Gettysburg by Colonel Francis E. Heath, a clerk from Waterville. He was wounded on July 3, and Lieutenant Colonel Henry Whitman took over the regiment.

Close to where you parked, on the right side of the road you will find two small markers indicating the reserve positions of the 3rd and 4th Maine. General George Meade's impressive statue and his headquarters cabin are also on this side of the road. As you stand, looking west to Seminary Ridge, less than a mile away, you can see General Lee's statue at the tree line. One can almost imagine 160 cannon firing as 12,000–13,000 Confederate soldiers marched across that deadly field in battle formation, little more than half returning after the failed attack.

At this point, you may want to wipe the tears from your eyes and take a lunch break. If not, continue on North Hancock Avenue, turning left and then right to go north on Steinwehr Avenue. This street has many places to dine and shop.

Going down Steinwehr Avenue, take the first right at the Taneytown Road. Park in the parking lot to the right and cross the street on foot to:

The National Cemetery, Cemetery Hill
Map Coordinates — 39.81754° N, 77.231854° W.

There, through the cemetery gates, you will find the Lincoln's Gettysburg Address Memorial. Walking to the west you will come to the burial sites, divided by states into lots, 104 Maine men are buried in Lot 15 (Map Coordinates — 39.8203270N, 77.2310430W).

On the eastern slope of the National Cemetery, near the Evergreen Cemetery fence, you will find the second day position of Hall's Second Maine Battery (Map Coordinates — 39.8182080N, 77.2314810W).

Return to your car and drive back down the Taneytown Road, taking a right at the light onto Steinwehr Avenue. Continue on Steinwehr Avenue until you come to the intersection with Baltimore Street (a gas station will be on the right). Turn a sharp right onto Baltimore Street, which will soon become Baltimore Pike (Rte. 97). You will soon find parking spaces on the right — park to find:

Oliver Otis Howard Statue — Cemetery Hill

Map Coordinates — 39.821948° N, 77.228877° W.

General Oliver Otis Howard was born in Leeds, Maine, in 1830. He graduated from both Bowdoin College and West Point. As you go to the other side of the monument you will notice his empty coat sleeve, having lost his arm at the Battle of Seven Pines in 1862. A deeply religious man, Howard received the thanks of Congress for selecting Cemetery Hill as the Union position during the Battle of Gettysburg.

Just a few paces away is General Winfield Scott Hancock's equestrian statue. Hancock was badly wounded during Pickett's Charge (as you can tell because one front leg is off the ground).

Back in the car, continue down the Baltimore Pike (you will go past the Evergreen Cemetery gate to the right) about ¹/₅ of a mile past the Hunt Avenue intersection. There on the left (or east) of the Pike you will find:

10th Maine Battalion Monument — Baltimore Pike

Map Coordinates – 39.811509° N, 77.220723° W.

The 10th Maine Regiment was mustered out of service early in 1863. However, 170 of the men had signed three-year papers so they were organized, under the leadership of Captain John Davis Beardsley, as a three-company battalion to serve as provost guard (policemen) for the headquarters of the Army of the Potomac. These men did perform some scouting duty and suffered no casualties during the battle.

Continue down Baltimore Pike for another ³/₁₀ of a mile, turning left onto the National Park

Service road marked for Culp's Hill (sometimes called Colonel Grove Avenue). You will soon come to Spangler's Spring. A natural spring to the southeast of Gettysburg at the south base of Culp's Hill, this area was held by each side during the battle. During the night of July 2, both sides filled their canteens from the spring.

Continue straight to Slocum Avenue, along this road you will find many monuments, mostly representing New York or Pennsylvania troops. The 137th New York monument is very interesting, as this regiment held at one time on July 2 the farthest right flank of the Union Army, just as the 20th Maine held the farthest left flank. The regiment's commander, Colonel David Ireland, is as much a hero of the battle as Joshua Chamberlain, yet receives very little credit. Perhaps because he died later in the war and did not have the chance to write several books about his service, as Chamberlain did.

As you continue on Slocum Avenue, there is a loop road to take to the right that takes you to the third battlefield observation tower. This gives a great view of Culp's Hill and Cemetery Hill to the northwest.

Back on Slocum Avenue you will come to a small knoll, now knows as Stevens's Knoll. Park here to find:

Stevens's 5th Maine Battery, Stevens's Knoll
Map Coordinates – 39.81935° N, 77.224564° W.

The 5th Maine Battery was commanded at the Battle of Gettysburg by Captain Greenlief Thurlow Stevens. The battery was held (Stop Number 3) on Seminary Ridge on the first day of the battle but moved to this position, where it was heavily engaged on July 2. Captain Stevens was wounded in both legs on July 2, and Lieutenant Edward N. Whittier took command. Whittier went on to be awarded the Medal of Honor for his actions at Fisher's Hill in 1864.

To the northwest from this position you can see the slope of Cemetery Hill quite clearly, guarded by the statues of Generals Howard and Hancock. To the rear of the 5th Maine monument is General Henry Slocum's statue, the head of 12th Corps (and self appointed commander of the right wing of the Army of the Potomac). The sculptor of Slocum's statue, Edward Clark Potter, later created the famous lions in front of the New York Public Library.

Continue on Slocum Avenue until you get back to the Baltimore Pike, turning right and continuing to the downtown traffic circle in Gettysburg. There, take the first right onto York Street (Rte. 30 East), at the second traffic light bear right onto the Hanover Road (Rte. 116). Continue for several miles, going over Rte. 15. After about $7/10$ of a mile you will see a marker on the left side of the road. Stop here (note — this is a fairly narrow and dangerous spot of the Hanover Road, use caution):

1st Maine Cavalry Monument, Hanover Road
Map Coordinates — 39.81795°N, 77.169235° W.

The 1st Maine Cavalry Regiment lost the greatest number killed in action of any cavalry regiment in the Army: fifteen officers and 159 enlisted men killed and mortally wounded; three officers and 341 enlisted men died of disease during the Civil War. At the Battle of Gettysburg, the regiment was held mostly in reserve. This beautiful monument on the south side of the cavalry battlefield was dedicated by the State of Maine in 1889.

From here the driving tour of Maine monuments at Gettysburg ends. If you continue down the Hanover Road to the left you will find East Cavalry Avenue, which will take you around the cavalry battlefield until you finally end up at the York Pike. Take a left here to return to downtown Gettysburg.

THIS MONUMENT COMMEMORATES THE SERVICES OF THE FIRST MAINE CAVALRY ON THIS BATTLE-FIELD, JULY 3, 1863. COL. C. H. SMITH, COMMANDING.

3RD BRIGADE, 2ND DIVISION, CAVALRY CORPS.

However, there is one more monument to find. Unfortunately, the monument is on private property along the Baltimore Pike. If you must see it, go to the information desk at the Gettysburg Visitor Center and ask a park ranger if he or she will give you a telephone number to call to make arrangements for a visit.

The 7th Maine monument is located on an old road known as Neill Avenue. Now unused, it is known as "the Lost Lane." Three other monuments, the 43rd New York, 49th New York, and the 61st Pennsylvania are also located on the lane. The 7th Maine monument is of beautiful white granite, second in beauty to only to the 17th Maine's monument on the battlefield. It is decorated with the Greek cross symbol of the 6th Corps, superimposed on a shield.

The commander of the regiment, Colonel Selden Connor helped design the monument. He, like Joshua Chamberlain, went on to become Governor of the State of

Maine. The regiment of 261 men, in six companies (the other companies were in Maine recruiting), as part of the 6th Corps, were held in reserve, taking only light casualties as skirmishers while protecting the rear of the Union Army against advance elements of Stuart's cavalry.

If you do have a chance to see this monument, understand that it is now in a working cow pasture — as the owner of the property will tell you, watch out for "Confederate landmines!"

FURTHER READING

NOTE: Rather than bore the reader with an exhaustive bibliography that nobody but the Ph.Ds will check, find below a list of my favorite books about the Civil War and the Battle of Gettysburg. Anyone who finishes reading these books should be considered a Civil War historian. It is interesting that 15 of the 52 books below were written before 1900, 18 were written between 1901 and 1990 (the date of the Ken Burns *Civil War* series), and 19 were written between 1991 and 2013, thus they represent a fairly balanced selection over the past 150 years of scholarship. The reader will probably note the author's preference for narrative historians such as Bruce Catton, Shelby Foote, and Bell I. Wiley, but, a warning: several of the books below are scholarly and deep while others are quite long. For example, when reading Drew Gilpin Faust's book, *This Republic of Suffering*, you must read each paragraph at least twice, it is worth it. Edward Tobie's book about the 1st Maine Cavalry, on the other hand, runs over 700 pages, so feel free to skim and skip. Most book critics and historians of the period agree that James M. McPherson's *Battle Cry of Freedom* and Edwin Coddington's study, *The Gettysburg Campaign*, published during the centennial of the battle in 1963, are the best comprehensive one-volume books ever written about the Civil War and the Battle of Gettysburg, so those would be a good place for the reader to start.

The Top Ten Books About the Civil War

1. *Battle Cry of Freedom,* by James M. McPherson (1988)

2. *A Stillness at Appomattox,* by Bruce Catton (1953)

3. *How the North Won: A Military History of the Civil War,* by Herman Hattaway and Archer Jones (1983)

4. *The Civil War,* (3 volumes) by Shelby Foote (1958-1974)

5. *The Destructive War: William Tecumseh Sherman, Stonewall Jackson and the Americans,* by Charles Royster (1992)

6. *Team of Rivals: The Political Genius of Abraham Lincoln,* by Doris Kearns Goodwin (2006)

7. *This Republic of Suffering: Death and the American Civil War,* by Drew Gilpin Faust (2008)

8. *Red Badge of Courage,* by Stephen Crane (1895)

9. *A Great Civil War: A Military and Political History, 1861-1865,* by Russell F. Weigley (2001)

10. (Tie) *The Life of Johnny Reb,* by Bell Irvin Wiley (1943)

10. (Tie) *The Life of Billy Yank,* by Bell Irvin Wiley (1952)

The Top Ten Books About Gettysburg

1. *The Gettysburg Campaign: A Study in Command,* by Edwin Coddington (1963)

2. *Gettysburg: The Second Day,* by Harry W. Pfanz (1998)

3. *Glory Road,* by Bruce Catton (1952)

4. *Gettysburg: A Journey in Time,* by William A. Frassanito (1996)

5. *The Killer Angels,* By Michael Shaara (1974)

6. *Gettysburg,* by Stephen Sears (2003)

7. *The First Day at Gettysburg: Essays on Confederate and Union Leadership,* edited by Gary W. Gallagher (1992)

8. *The Maps of Gettysburg,* by Bradley M. Gottfried (2007)

9. *A Field Guide to Gettysburg,* by Carol Reardon and Tom Vossler (2013)

10. *The Gettysburg Nobody Knows,* by Gabor S. Boritt (1999)

Top Ten Books About Maine During the Civil War

1. *The Twentieth Maine: A Volunteer Regiment in the Civil War,* by John J. Pullen (1957)

2. *Stand Firm Ye Boys from Maine: The 20th Maine and the Gettysburg Campaign,* by Thomas A. Desjardin (1995)

3. *Red Diamond Regiment: The 17th Maine Regiment, 1862-1865,* by William B. Jordan, Jr. (1996)

4. *No Rich Men's Sons: The Sixth Maine Volunteer Infantry,* by James H. Mundy (1994)

5. *The Sixteenth Maine Regiment in the War of the Rebellion,* by Abner Ralph Small (1886)

6. *Through Blood and Fire at Gettysburg: General Joshua Chamberlain and the 20th Maine,* by Joshua Lawrence Chamberlain (1877, reprinted in 1995)

7. *History of the First Maine Cavalry, 1861-1865,* by Edward P. Tobie (1887)

8. *Army Life: a Private's Reminiscences of the Civil War,* by Theodore Gerrish (1882)

9. *A Shower of Stars: The Medal of Honor and the 27th Maine,* by John J. Pullen (1966)

10. (Tie) *A Distant War Comes Home: Maine in the Civil War Era,* by Donald W. Beattie, Rodney M. Cole, and Charles G. Waugh, 1996

10. (Tie) *Following the Greek Cross, or Memories of the Sixth Army Corps,* by Thomas W. Hyde (1894, reprinted in 2005)

Top Ten Reference Books

1. *The War of the Rebellion: a Compilation of the Official Records of the Union and Confederate Armies,* Government Printing Office, 128 volumes, (1881-1901)

2. *A Compendium of the War of the Rebellion,* by Frederick H. Dyer (1908)

3. *Annual Report of the Adjutant General of the State of Maine,* by Adjutant General's Office, 11 volumes, (1860-1871)

4. *Maine at Gettysburg: Report of Maine Commissioners,* Prepared by the Executive Committee, (1898).

5. *Alphabetical Index of Maine Volunteers, etc., Mustered Into the Service of the United States During the War of 1861,* by Adjutant General's Office, (1867)

6. *Regimental Losses in the American Civil War 1861-1865*, by William F. Fox (1889)

7. *Numbers and Losses in the Civil War in America, 1861-1865,* by Thomas L. Livermore (1901)

8. *Historical Times Illustrated Encyclopedia of the Civil War,* edited by Patricia L. Faust (1986)

9. *The Civil War Day By Day: An Almanac, 1861-1865,* by E. B. Long and Barbara Long (1985)

10. *The Civil War Dictionary,* by Mark M. Boatner (1959)

Top Ten Civil War Books I Read Over and Over

1. *American Heritage Picture History of the Civil War,* by Bruce Catton (1960) — This was my first Civil War book, I basically have worn it out. Try to get the 1960 edition, it is much better that the 2001 reprint.

2. *The Personal Memoirs of Ulysses S. Grant,* by Ulysses S. Grant (1885) — This has to be the best autobiography ever written.

3. *Landscape Turned Red,* by Stephen W. Sears (1983) — By far the best account of the Battle of Antietam.

4. *Stonewall Jackson: The Man, The Soldier, The Legend,* by James Robertson (1997) — I had a chance to work with Mr. Robertson for a few days at the National Civil War Museum, so I have a signed copy of this great book.

5. *Confederates in the Attic: Dispatches from the Unfinished Civil War,* by Tony Horwitz (1998) — Having traipsed through the underbrush of many Southern battlefields with other Civil War nuts, I appreciate this book, it cracks me up every time I read it.

6. *Lincoln,* by David Herbert Donald (1996) — there are probably as many books about Abraham Lincoln as there are about the Battle of Gettysburg. This is my favorite one-volume study, although I do also like Gore Vidal's book about Lincoln.

7. *Embattled Courage: The Experience of Combat in the American Civil War,* by Gerald F. Linderman (1987) — An excellent study of courage and the psychosocial effects of the Civil War upon the soldiers who fought in it.

8. *What They Fought For, 1861-1865 and For Cause and Comrades,*
    by James M. McPherson (1994, 1997) — Although short, these books sum it
    all up for me.

9. *The Passing of the Armies: An Account of the Final Campaign of the Army of
    the Potomac,* by Joshua Lawrence Chamberlain (1915) — Published a year after
    he died, Professor Chamberlain did have a way with words.

10. *Mary Chesnut's Civil War,* edited by C. Vann Woodward (1981) — Pick up this
    book and thumb to any of the 880 pages to find amazing insights about the war
    and its leaders written by a woman from the upper-class planter elite.

INDEX

Illustrations are indicated by italicized page numbers

INDEX OF MAPS